Corporate Bond Markets in Asia

CHALLENGES AND OPPORTUNITIES FOR GROWTH COMPANIES

OECD
BETTER POLICIES FOR BETTER LIVES

This work is published under the responsibility of the Secretary-General of the OECD. The opinions expressed and arguments employed herein do not necessarily reflect the official views of the Member countries of the OECD.

This document, as well as any data and map included herein, are without prejudice to the status of or sovereignty over any territory, to the delimitation of international frontiers and boundaries and to the name of any territory, city or area.

Please cite this publication as:
OECD (2024), *Corporate Bond Markets in Asia: Challenges and Opportunities for Growth Companies*, OECD Capital Market Series, OECD Publishing, Paris, https://doi.org/10.1787/96192f4a-en.

ISBN 978-92-64-53441-4 (print)
ISBN 978-92-64-64729-9 (PDF)
ISBN 978-92-64-49739-9 (HTML)

OECD Capital Market Series
ISSN 3006-5801 (online)

Revised version, March 2025
Details of revisions available at: https://www.oecd.org/about/publishing/corrigenda.htm

Photo credits: Cover © Thirawatana Phaisalratana/Getty Images.

Corrigenda to OECD publications may be found at: https://www.oecd.org/en/publications/support/corrigenda.html.

Foreword

This report offers a comprehensive review of the current state of corporate bond markets in 18 Asian jurisdictions and Australia. It also outlines key policy considerations on how to improve the functioning of corporate bond markets in the region, including how to make these markets more accessible to growth companies. The information provided in the report has been gathered through a survey prepared by the OECD and responded by 19 national regulators, as well as from OECD databases and desktop research.

This report is the result of a project carried out by the OECD with the financial support of the Ministry of Foreign Affairs of the Republic of Korea. The main objective of this project is to support the sustainable development of Asian economies by providing policy considerations on how to improve their policies and frameworks for corporate finance and corporate governance, specifically focusing on the conditions for market-based financing via corporate bonds for large and growth companies.

Against this background, the report formulates policy considerations to improve the conditions for market-based financing via corporate bonds for companies in Asia in the first chapter, and the remaining chapters provide an in-depth overview of the corporate bond markets landscape in the region, their functioning and the main challenges.

The report benefits from the discussions at the 2023 OECD-Asia Roundtable on Corporate Governance in Malaysia, held in October 2023. Additionally, the policy considerations in the report were discussed with regulators and stakeholders from the region during a webinar held on 6 February 2024. The report was also shared for comments with experts participating in the 2023 OECD-Asia Roundtable on Corporate Governance and participants to the webinar. The authors are grateful for the participation in the webinar of the following regulators and stakeholders: Malen Pov (Cambodia, SERC); Alieta Lestariwandari (Indonesia, OJK); Gentha Wardana (Indonesia, OJK); Yusak Liestia Ramagit Setiawan (Indonesia, OJK); Kenta Fukami (Japan, FSA); Shu Asai (Japan, FSA); Jaemin Kim (Korea, FSC); Whayoung Jung (Korea Capital Market Institute); Kaveena Maniam (Malaysia, SEC); Emma A. Valencia (Philippines, SEC); Alex Huang (Chinese Taipei, Securities and Futures Bureau); Ada Ing (Thailand, Thai Reinsurance PCL); Duy Phan (Viet Nam, Hanoi Stock Exchange); Kiên Trần Trọng (Viet Nam, Hanoi Stock Exchange); Duong Hoang (Viet Nam, SSC); Mai Nguyen (Viet Nam, SSC); Satoru Yamadera (ADB); Philippe Dirckx (ASIFMA); Haifeng Xue (Moody's); Yongjoo Lee (Permanent Delegation of Korea to the OECD); Prof. Aurelio Gurrea Martinez (Singapore Management University); Richard Dyason (The Institute of International Auditors Singapore).

The report also benefits from written feedback received from the Financial Services Agency of Japan, Monetary Authority of Singapore, Thai Securities and Exchange Commission, Clifford Chance, Moody's and Prof. Aurelio Gurrea Martinez.

The report was prepared by Anna Dawson, Kyo Maruyama, Tugba Mulazimoglu, Caroline Roulet and Yun Tang under the supervision of Alejandra Medina, all from the Capital Markets and Financial Institutions Division of the OECD Directorate for Financial and Enterprise Affairs.

Table of contents

FIGURES

TABLES

Follow OECD Publications on:

https://twitter.com/OECD

https://www.facebook.com/theOECD

https://www.linkedin.com/company/organisation-eco-cooperation-development-organisation-cooperation-developpement-eco/

https://www.youtube.com/user/OECDiLibrary

https://www.oecd.org/newsletters/

Acronyms and abbreviations

ABMI	Asian Bond Markets Initiative
ACRAA	Association of Credit Rating Agencies in Asia
ADB	Asian Development Bank
ASEAN	Association of Southeast Asian Nations
CBO	collateralised bond obligation
CCRS	Corporate Credit Rating System
CDS	credit default swap
CGT	capital gains tax
CPI	Consumer Price Index
CRAs	credit rating agencies
ESMA	European Securities and Markets Authority
FIBEN	Fichier bancaire des entreprises
FSB	Financial Stability Board
GDP	gross domestic product
HKMA	Hong Kong Monetary Authority
IMF	International Monetary Fund
IOSCO	International Organization of Securities Commissions
KOSME	Korea SMEs and Startups Agency
LOLA	Lodge and Launch
LSEG	London Stock Exchange Group
MARC	Malaysian Rating Corporation Berhad
MAS	Monetary Authority of Singapore
OECD	Organisation for Economic Co-operation and Development
OJK	Financial Services Authority of Indonesia
OTC	over-the-counter
P2P	peer-to-peer financing
SBSS	Start-up Business Scoring System
SC Malaysia	Malaysian Securities Commission
SCORE	SME Competitiveness Rating for Enhancement
SEBI	Securities and Exchange Board of India
SESS	Small Enterprise Scoring System
SME	small and medium-sized enterprise
SRI	Sustainable and Responsible Investment
WHT	withholding tax
SBSS	Start-up Business Scoring System

Executive summary

Following the Asian financial crisis, regional authorities recognised the importance of well-functioning capital markets and took steps to facilitate the use of market-based financing. Consequently, reforms were introduced in many jurisdictions to develop corporate bond markets as a source of financing for corporations and significant progress has been observed since then. Still, the level of development of corporate bond markets differs in the region and in most jurisdictions only large, high-quality issuers can issue bonds. In general, growth companies still face substantive barriers to access this type of financing.

This report formulates policy considerations to further develop corporate bond markets and to facilitate access by growth companies. This is informed by an overview of Asian corporate bond markets, including their functioning and challenges, and is based on information provided by 19 regulators via a survey, OECD databases and desktop research. Some of the key findings are listed below:

Corporate bond markets in Asia have grown significantly, however bank financing still dominates in the region. Corporate bond issuance has significantly increased in Asian markets, from representing 16% of the global issuance in 2000, to 49% in 2022. Corporate bond markets have also been offering increasing financing opportunities for growth companies. The issuance by growth companies increased from USD 5.7 billion in 2000 to USD 33.3 billion in 2022. Despite the rapid development of both public equity and corporate bond markets in Asia, corporations still rely heavily on bank financing, with market-based financing taking a secondary role. In Asia, bank credit extended to non-financial companies stands at 143% of GDP, much higher than the global number at 96%.

Corporate bond markets in Asia are at different stages of development. While some jurisdictions have developed their corporate bond markets for large and growth companies, some markets are at a very early stage of development where only large, highly-rated companies have access to financing. Relatedly, very few jurisdictions have exemptions or programmes to facilitate growth companies' access to corporate bond markets. Indeed, 13 jurisdictions have implemented at least one measure to increase overall access to corporate bond markets, but not specifically targeting growth companies.

A well-functioning government bond market is essential to develop other securities markets. A domestic liquid, risk-free yield curve allows the pricing of risky securities, including corporate bonds. Not all Asian jurisdictions have a well-developed government bond market, and even where the market exists, there are significant differences in the size, depth and liquidity of these markets. Corporate bonds can be listed and traded on the stock exchange in 16 jurisdictions, while an OTC market operates in 13 jurisdictions.

Many jurisdictions have improved their regulatory frameworks. A well-functioning corporate bond market requires a robust regulatory framework that ensures investor protection, maintains market integrity and mitigates systemic risks. Legal and regulatory provisions in most jurisdictions require registration or approval by regulators, with some jurisdictions mandating both. Common requirements include submitting a prospectus, historical financial statements and ongoing disclosure of information. Recurrent corporate bond issuers often benefit from streamlined processes. Regarding bondholder rights, trustee appointments are common, with 14 jurisdictions mandating this for corporate bond issues, while all require disclosure of material covenant-related information. Additionally, many jurisdictions have improved bankruptcy procedures to bolster creditor rights and facilitate corporate debt restructuring. However, only a few jurisdictions' insolvency frameworks include components such as out-of-court restructuring frameworks, hybrid regimes and fast-track procedures for SMEs. Applying necessary requirements for bonds issued to qualified investors, eliminating overly burdensome requirements and tailoring proportional requirements for growth companies should be a priority to further improve corporate bond markets in the region.

Asian corporate bond markets are characterised by low secondary market liquidity. A liquid market ensures an efficient price formation process, improves investor confidence and contributes to the overall functioning of capital markets. Corporate bond markets in Asia are characterised by low liquidity, which is identified as the most important barrier to developing these markets. Despite regulatory provisions in several jurisdictions, inactive market makers and lack of investors are among the key factors hindering liquidity.

There are challenges to credit rating assessments. Difficulties evaluating the creditworthiness of companies undermine investors' ability to accurately evaluate risks and affect their willingness to invest. The existence of various credit rating opinions enriches the information available to investors. All jurisdictions in Asia have registered at least one credit rating agency. Alternative credit rating systems have only been adopted in three jurisdictions. Nevertheless, the assessment of the creditworthiness of companies was identified as a key barrier to support and develop corporate bond markets in Asia.

A lack of investors is a significant barrier to the development of corporate bond markets in Asia. The composition and diversity of the investor base play a pivotal role in shaping the dynamism and resilience of corporate bond markets. However, several jurisdictions identified the lack of investors, as well as investor's lack of interest, as major barriers for the development of corporate bond markets. In Asia, institutional investors are relatively large, representing a significant share of the world's total assets of pension funds and insurance companies. Therefore, they have substantial investment capacity to play a more significant role in Asian capital markets.

Tax treatment of corporate bonds is broadly similar in structure in Asia. In most jurisdictions companies are allowed to a tax deduction for the interest paid to corporate bonds investors and other expenses. From the investor's perspective, it is common to pay tax on the interest received from holding corporate bonds while capital gains are taxed in only 14 jurisdictions. A withholding tax for foreign investors is generally applied unless there is a double taxation agreement, which is common in many jurisdictions. However, there are differences in the rates and conditions applied. Overall, the use of tax exemptions to help attract issuers and investors is not common in Asia.

Targeted policies or programmes to support growth companies' access to bond markets are not common. Most measures implemented in the region aim to increase the overall access to corporate bond markets and are not targeted to growth companies. Only a few jurisdictions with more mature markets have implemented targeted policies to facilitate growth companies' access to corporate bond markets and, in general, growth companies still face substantive barriers to access this type of financing. Only four jurisdictions waive certain requirements or procedures for growth companies.

Against this background, this report formulates policy considerations for authorities in Asia to further develop corporate bond markets and enhance growth companies' access to these markets. The policy considerations outlined in this report are centred around three main objectives. First, they aim to ensure that regional markets first develop the pre-requisites for well-functioning corporate bond markets. Second, they aim to develop the corporate bond market for large firms first. And third, they target the facilitation of growth companies' access to corporate bond markets. Ensuring the enabling factors are in place and that the bond market is working for large companies, could provide a robust foundation for credibility and trust in the market, and foster a culture that encourages the subsequent participation by growth companies.

The policy considerations are grouped into the following seven areas: pre-requisites for well-functioning corporate bond markets; appropriate regulatory and supervisory framework; adequate and independent credit risk assessment for companies all sizes; improved secondary market liquidity; diversified investor base; instruments to attract a large pool of investors and diversify risk; and role of government and other initiatives.

Summary of policy considerations

1. Pre-requisites for well-functioning corporate bond markets	
Code of conduct	Encourage adherence to and enforcement of a robust code of conduct among market participants to ensure the proper functioning of the marketplace.
Market infrastructure	Improve systems and venues for clearing and settlement systems to meet the needs of a wider range of investors.
Market intermediaries	Ensure market intermediaries have sufficient technical capacity and knowledge since they play a key role in safeguarding the robustness of the market infrastructure, and in any listing or trading processes.
Alternative trading systems	Ensure the availability of alternative trading systems.
Government bond markets	Prioritise the development of a robust government bond market for the development of wider capital markets. This could include improving the liquidity of the yield curve and extending its maturity.
Capital allocation and the mobilisation of savings	Ensure efficient capital allocation and the mobilisation of savings in the economy. Additional efforts could be directed to promote a savings culture and increase savings rates in the economy.
2. Appropriate regulatory and supervisory framework	
Regulatory and supervisory frameworks	Implement robust regulatory and supervisory frameworks and strengthen investor protection efforts.
Approval or registration of bond issues	Reduce the time for approval or registration of bond issues.
Template for corporate bond terms	Develop and implement a template for corporate bond terms to facilitate comparability and reduce execution time, in particular for corporate bond issuances by growth companies.
Frequent issuers	Facilitate the issuance process for frequent issuers, by allowing them to follow simplified procedures and/or issue a simplified prospectus or a generic prospectus.
Exemptions in the corporate bond issuance process	Consider including certain exemptions in the corporate bond issuance process such as waiving or decreasing the number of historical financial statements for newly established corporations or permitting a simplified prospectus.
Special frameworks for growth companies	Consider creating special frameworks for growth companies with less stringent requirements, cost-effective issuance processes and tax advantages.
Bondholder rights, insolvency regulations	Introduce systems that facilitate bondholders to exercise their rights. Authorities could consider enhancing bankruptcy and restructuring regulations.
3. Adequate and independent credit risk assessment for companies all sizes	
Credit rating assessments	Ensure the existence of well-functioning diverse credit rating assessments for corporate bonds and other debt securities at affordable prices for companies all sizes.
Accurate, reliable and comparable opinions	Ensure credit rating agencies provide markets with accurate, reliable and comparable opinions. Moreover, they should follow rigorous standards, use solid methodologies, disclose their methodologies and be independent from market actors.
Domestic rating agencies	Support the establishment of domestic rating agencies to increase the availability of credit ratings assessment in markets where domestic rating agencies are not established or still developing.
Alternative credit rating systems	Consider creating an alternative credit rating system for growth companies to provide credit risk assessments to the market.
Incentives for growth companies	Consider introducing incentives specifically for growth companies, such as covering the full or partial cost of obtaining a credit rating to issue a corporate bond.
Harmonisation of the credit rating practices	Encourage active participation in regional initiatives aimed at harmonising and improving the quality of the credit rating practices of CRAs in Asia to be in line with IOSCO Code of Conduct Fundamentals for CRAs.
4. Improved secondary market liquidity	
Marketplaces	Establish a dedicated segment on the stock exchange with less stringent requirements and/or making it only dedicated to qualified investors.
Price transparency	Ensure a level of price transparency that promotes efficient price discovery in corporate bond markets.

Reference pricing	Consider introducing systems to provide reference pricing and/or ensuring dissemination of market prices to the market.
Market making mechanism	Ensure a well-functioning market making mechanism to support secondary market liquidity in corporate bond markets.
Research on growth companies	Consider establishing a mechanism that provides independent quantitative research on growth companies to market participants at no cost.
Trading fees, and the tax treatment of corporate bonds	Ensure that trading fees, the tax treatment of corporate bonds and their related procedures do not discourage participation in the corporate bond market.
5. Diversified investor base	
Institutional investors	Assess the legal, regulatory and institutional framework governing institutional investors, taking into account its impact on the capital available to growth companies. Continue reforming the pension systems and supporting the development of insurance corporations in the region.
Foreign investors	Address regulatory obstacles, the cost of accessing the market and taxation issues for foreign investors.
Retail investors	Promote the direct or indirect participation of retail investors while ensuring the risks taken by these investors are well-understood and properly managed.
Financial literacy	Increase the financial literacy of retail investors.
6. Instruments to attract a large pool of investors and diversify risk	
Securitisation	Introduce a securitisation mechanism to promote the development of corporate bond markets for growth companies.
Guarantees	Establish a guarantee scheme to support growth companies' access to market-based financing.
Derivative markets	Continue developing the derivative markets to provide risk management tools to investors and intermediaries investing in corporate bonds.
Qualified investors	Develop corporate bond markets for growth companies to qualified investors first.
7. Role of government and other initiatives	
Reform agenda	Establish a comprehensive reform agenda to promote growth companies' access to corporate bond markets.
Taxation framework	Review the taxation framework to support growth companies' access to financing and simplify tax declaration and payment procedures.
Segment for growth companies	Establish a dedicated segment for growth companies on the stock exchange using proportional listing requirements and less stringent rules, while ensuring appropriate investor protection.
Industry-led bodies or associations	Enhance the role of industry-led bodies or associations in corporate bond markets.
Financial education	Establish dedicated and targeted financial education or awareness campaign to inform corporate executives and other relevant actors about the opportunities of corporate bond financing.

1 Assessment and policy considerations

This chapter provides an assessment of various factors influencing the functioning of corporate bond markets, including the regulatory and supervisory frameworks, credit risk assessment, secondary market liquidity, investor base and instruments to attract a large pool of investors. Additionally, it examines the government's role in promoting these markets. Under each of the above-mentioned areas the chapter also formulates policy considerations for Asian regulators addressing the key challenges identified.

Small and medium-sized enterprises (SMEs) represent the vast majority of firms in Asia. In 2021, micro, small and medium-sized enterprises represented on average 98.9% of all corporations and were responsible for 46.1% of employment (ADB, 2022[1]). Within SMEs, growth companies are usually defined as medium-sized companies with the potential to rapidly expand, create jobs, increase productivity, push the frontiers of innovation and challenge the status quo with new products and business models. Therefore, these companies play an important role in stimulating the economy by being at the front of innovation. However, in many bank-dominated Asian economies, growth companies still face substantive barriers to access financing. Due to a lack of history and other information, growth companies are generally required to provide large collaterals or are charged higher lending interest rates compared to large established firms (Yoshino and Taghizadeh-Hesary, 2018[2]). Moreover, bank lending is typically short-term not providing enough support for long-term investment by these companies.

High dependence on bank lending increases the fragility of the corporate sector by amplifying the impact of external shocks, especially when banks reduce their risk tolerance and tighten lending conditions. This was evident in the global financial crisis, where the downturn was greater in bank-based financing systems than in market-based systems (Gambacorta, Yang and Tsatsaronis, 2014[3]). Moreover, underdeveloped capital markets with few opportunities for long-term financing also contributed to the spread of the Asian financial crisis. Importantly, the significant use of bank financing also drives the accumulation of non-performing loans. Although non-performing loans ratio have been stable and low in Asia since 2005, the reliance on bank loans exposes economies to the risk of a rapid deterioration in loan quality, possibly locking up resources in unproductive businesses (OECD, 2022[4]).

The growth of capital markets, especially corporate bond markets, can bolster sustainable growth for Asian firms by facilitating long-term financing and enhancing their resilience. Since the Asian financial crisis, regional authorities have acknowledged the significance of robust capital markets and have taken measures to reduce dependence on bank funding. Consequently, various reforms have been implemented across Asian jurisdictions to foster corporate bond markets. Although Asian firms have increasingly utilised corporate bond markets, their development varies across jurisdictions. Notably, these markets primarily cater to a handful of large companies, as only a limited number possess the size and reputation to issue bonds.

A well-functioning corporate bond market requires various factors to operate effectively. Initially, adequate market infrastructure, markets offering price transparency and discovery, and deep and liquid government bond markets, are essential. The presence of robust corporate governance frameworks and a code of conduct for market participants are also enabling factors. Additionally, fostering the development of corporate bond markets requires authorities to ensure the existence of appropriate regulatory and supervisory frameworks, adequate and independent credit risk assessment for companies of all sizes, improved secondary market liquidity, a diversified investor base, and instruments to attract a large pool of investors and diversify risk. All these aspects will be discussed in the following sections.

1.1. Pre-requisites for well-functioning corporate bond markets

To operate effectively, corporate bond markets rely on several key factors. Firstly, they require an open financial market with robust infrastructure and deep, liquid government bond markets to efficiently allocate capital and mobilise savings. Once these foundational elements are established, facilitating access for larger companies to corporate bond markets builds credibility and trust while fostering a culture that encourages participation by growth companies.

Safe and efficient financial **market infrastructures** contribute to maintaining and promoting financial stability. These infrastructures, which encompass trading systems, central counterparties (CCPs) and securities settlement systems (SSS) are instrumental in enabling market participants to fulfil their obligations with confidence and in a timely manner. Marketplaces are also part of the market infrastructure.

In particular, off-exchange markets such as **alternative trading systems (ATSs) and multilateral trading facilities (MTFs)** function in many developed markets following non-discretionary rules. These markets play a significant role alongside stock exchanges in facilitating trading activities. Although the predominant platform for trading debt securities is over-the-counter (OTC), listing bonds on stock exchanges can provide essential safeguards for investors while enhancing transparency and the price discovery process.

The development of robust **government bond markets** is essential within capital markets for several reasons. Firstly, government bonds are highly liquid and considered risk-free instruments at the local level, and therefore used as a benchmark for pricing various financial instruments including corporate bonds. A well-developed government bond market contributes to overall market liquidity and stability, and is pivotal for the proper functioning of capital markets, facilitating the smooth transmission of monetary policy and fostering investor confidence in the broader financial system.

Some of the important components of a well-developed government bond market include extending the yield curve, informing the public regularly about the calendar of issuances to improve transparency, increasing the disclosure of information on public debt issuance and statistics, holding regular meetings with dealers, institutional investors and rating agencies, introducing a system of primary dealers, and establishing a repurchase (repo) market for the government bond market. Each of these features plays a crucial role in enhancing the efficiency and effectiveness of the market. Extending the yield curve, for instance, provides a broader range of investment options for market participants, while issuance calendars and increased transparency contribute to better-informed decision making and improved market confidence. Regular engagements with key stakeholders foster communication and understanding, which promotes a healthy and responsive market environment. Introducing primary dealers and establishing a repo market further bolsters liquidity, enabling smoother trading and facilitating effective monetary policy implementation.

Moreover, a well-developed government bond market is closely interconnected with a robust **money market**. A liquid money market is imperative for facilitating short-term borrowing and lending, providing a crucial avenue for market actors to manage liquidity efficiently. Additionally, it plays a key role in the transmission of monetary policy, allowing central banks to influence interest rates and maintain both price stability and financial stability within the broader economic framework. Thus, the interconnectedness between well-developed government bond markets and money markets is instrumental in fostering a resilient and dynamic financial ecosystem.

Efficient **capital allocation and mobilisation of savings** are primary objectives of capital markets. A robust capital market effectively connects savers with entities in need of capital, fostering a dynamic environment for wealth creation and efficient resource allocation ensuring that savings are channelled toward productive investments. However, some of the main elements required for the integrity and functionality of broader capital markets are the liberalisation of interest rates and capital movements. Liberalisation of interest rates ensures they reflect a more accurate picture of the market conditions, while unrestricted capital movements enhance market efficiency and investor confidence by allowing capital to flow freely. In the mobilisation of savings, institutional and retail investors are important players, each contributing uniquely to the market's depth and breadth (discussed further under the Section 1.5).

Policy considerations:

- Encourage adherence to and enforcement of a robust code of conduct among market participants to ensure the proper functioning of the marketplace. This with the aim to promote fairness, transparency and integrity, fostering trust among market participants and ensuring the proper functioning of the marketplace.
- Improve systems and venues for clearing and settlement systems to meet the needs of a wider range of investors.

- Ensure market intermediaries have sufficient technical capacity and knowledge since they play a key role in safeguarding the robustness of the market infrastructure, and in any listing or trading processes.
- Ensure the availability of alternative trading systems. This could help companies to gain familiarity with the capital market environment and gain exposure to a larger investor base.
- Prioritise the development of a robust government bond market for the development of wider capital markets. This could include improving the liquidity of the yield curve and extending its maturity. To enhance transparency, announcing an issuance calendar and having regular meetings with primary dealers in the government bond market could improve communication and improve market confidence.
- Ensure efficient capital allocation and the mobilisation of savings in the economy. Additional efforts could be directed to promote a savings culture and increase savings rates in the economy. In this respect, authorities could consider progressively removing any barriers to the movement of capital, while providing flexibility to cope with situations of economic and financial instability as recommended by the OECD Code of Liberalisation of Capital Movements (OECD, 2023[5]). Additional efforts could be directed to promote a savings culture and increase savings rates in the economy with the help of policies on financial education, saving instruments and supportive policy measures.

1.2. Appropriate regulatory and supervisory framework

Regulatory and supervisory frameworks play a crucial role in fostering the development of robust corporate bond markets. They should be designed to ensure investor protection, maintain market integrity and mitigate systemic risks in corporate bond markets. While integrating these elements, it is important that regulatory requirements do not create unnecessary impediments on companies' use of corporate bonds and investors' investment in corporate bonds. This consideration is especially critical for growth companies, given their limited resources and capacity to comply with regulatory requirements.

According to the OECD Survey, legal and regulatory provisions in most jurisdictions require registration or approval by regulators, with some jurisdictions mandating both. Common requirements include **submitting a prospectus, historical financial statements and ongoing disclosure of information**. The prospectus provides crucial information for investors about the securities that companies are issuing and the issuing company itself, and it is required in the 19 jurisdictions. Setting a short timeframe for prospectus approval enables corporations to get a clearer outlook on their issuance schedule. Two-thirds of the surveyed jurisdictions set a time frame within their regulatory frameworks for the regulator's approval process. Among these jurisdictions, the average time for the regulator's approval is around 40 days, with a varying time period across jurisdictions.

Introducing **a template for corporate bond terms** could provide companies clear guidance on the necessary requirements for issuing corporate bonds facilitating the procedure. This template can be particularly beneficial for growth companies, which often face constraints in financial resources and technical capacity. A template could additionally contribute to a more precise evaluation of credit risk and improve investors' understanding about the corporate bond markets in general. However, these terms still need the oversight of regulators, and it is crucial to ensure that a template does not constrain the issuers' flexibility in terms of the features that bond contracts could offer.

One common practice in corporate bond markets is to facilitate **the issuance process for frequent issuers**. In Asia, the majority of jurisdictions have a streamlined process for recurrent corporate bond issuers. These processes include allowing issuers to follow simplified procedures, to issue a simplified prospectus or a generic prospectus. Certain **exemptions** in the corporate bond issuance process could promote growth company's access to market-based financing. However, such exemptions are not common among the surveyed jurisdictions. Only four jurisdictions[1] waive certain requirements or procedures for growth companies.

Additionally, **specific measures** have been implemented in the region **to promote access to corporate bond markets**. It is noteworthy that measures tailored for growth companies are not prevalent in the region. Where they do exist, these measures generally aim to increase overall access to corporate bond markets by both large and growth companies.

Given that **bondholders** are often dispersed, challenges may arise in effectively **exercising their rights**, especially in insolvency procedures. Bondholders' involvement becomes particularly significant in major decisions for the company following a default or other covenant violation. While mainly targeting the corporate bonds of listed issuers, the revised G20/OECD Principles of Corporate Governance state that "the exercise of the rights of bondholders of publicly traded companies should be facilitated" (OECD, 2023[6]).

Insolvency systems are associated with an increase in the general availability and cost of credit, and a higher recovery rate for creditors (World Bank, 2014[7]). For a formal bankruptcy process to be effective, well-designed insolvency laws governing formal procedures for financially distressed companies are crucial. Notably, the efficacy of an insolvency framework is heavily contingent on the efficiency of the judicial system within which it operates. Many Asian jurisdictions have improved their bankruptcy procedures to strengthen creditor rights and facilitate the process of corporate debt restructuring. However, the OECD Survey showed that the insolvency frameworks of only a small number of Asian jurisdictions have components such as out-of-court restructuring frameworks, hybrid restructuring regimes and fast-track reorganisation and liquidation procedures for SMEs.

Another component of corporate bond markets that supports the enforcement of the bond terms and protects bondholder rights is **the bond trustee structure**. Trustees' duties are mainly to ensure timely bond interest payments and safeguard investor interests in the event of the issuer's default. While the exact scope of a trustee's activities is generally contractually defined, policymakers may enact regulation regarding the eligibility of a trustee and its duties prior to and during a default.

Policy considerations:

- Implement robust regulatory and supervisory frameworks and strengthen investor protection efforts.
- Reduce the time for approval or registration of bond issues. In this respect, authorities could further evaluate reducing the approval time for privately placed bonds, considering the capacities of investors already assessing the relevant risks. It could also be important to improve the level of technical skills and expertise of the regulator to effectively review corporate bond market processes.
- Develop and implement a template for corporate bond terms to facilitate comparability and reduce execution time, in particular for corporate bond issuances by growth companies. Companies also could attach a sheet where they report which terms they comply with and explain on those they do not comply. In this respect, the role of industry-led bodies or associations could be considered in preparing these contract templates.
- Facilitate the issuance process for frequent issuers, by allowing them to follow simplified procedures and/or issue a simplified prospectus or a generic prospectus.
- Consider including certain exemptions in the corporate bond issuance process such as waiving or decreasing the number of historical financial statements for newly established corporations or permitting a simplified prospectus. In particular, waiving the submission of a prospectus for small and privately placed bonds could be considered.

- Consider creating special frameworks for growth companies with less stringent requirements, cost-effective issuance processes and tax advantages.
- Introduce systems that facilitate bondholders to exercise their rights. This may involve incorporating provisions in the corporate governance framework and relevant regulation related to the trustee structure to ensure its efficient functioning, and on how to facilitate co-ordination among bondholders and their participation in any required voting.
- Authorities could consider enhancing bankruptcy and restructuring regulations. In particular, if lacking, out-of-court restructuring frameworks, hybrid restructuring regimes, fast-track reorganisation and liquidation for SMEs could be integrated to the insolvency frameworks for better functioning corporate bond markets.

1.3. Adequate and independent credit risk assessment for companies all sizes

Credit risk assessments of companies is an important tool for investors to understand and assess the risks involved in corporate bonds. A credit rating agency (CRA) uses a variety of public and non-public information to assess the creditworthiness of the issuer and formulates an opinion in an accessible and simple form. In general, easy and affordable access to get a credit rating and familiarity with the rating process significantly increases companies' ability to use long-term debt securities (Çelik, Demirtaş and Isaksson, 2020[8]). According to the OECD Survey results, domestic and regional CRAs are operating in all jurisdictions, and alternative credit rating systems have been developed in some Asian jurisdictions. Importantly, the majority of Asian jurisdictions identified the assessment of the creditworthiness of companies as a main barrier to the development of corporate bond markets.

As credit ratings are only the opinion of the credit rating agency, it is important to **ensure the accuracy, reliability, comparability and independence** of the credit ratings. The availability of a range of rating providers in the market can enhance the credit risk assessment process while at the same time deepening the general understanding of credit risk in the markets. The requirement to have at least two credit ratings for corporate bond issuances could increase confidence and trust by market participants. Market confidence could be further improved by mandating rating agencies to publish their methodologies and historical transition and default rates of their credit rating categories in accordance with IOSCO Code of Conduct Fundamentals for Credit Rating Agencies (IOSCO, 2015[9]). This information could also assist to evaluate the performance of CRAs by investors and other users of credit ratings. In addition, rating actions by CRAs need to be timely and forward-looking.

Obtaining a credit rating for a bond issuance from CRAs typically demands technical expertise to understand and navigate the involved processes, which growth companies may lack. Additionally, considering the costs associated, it can also be unaffordable for smaller issuers to obtain a credit rating. To address this issue and support market-based financing for growth companies, some jurisdictions have introduced **alternative credit rating systems** where an institution other than a CRA provides rating services. However, while all CRAs share the common goal of assessing credit risk, alternative rating systems could exhibit differences in their methodologies. These differences emphasise the need for careful consideration and evaluation of the diverse approaches and capabilities inherent in alternative credit rating systems.

In Asia, efforts have been made to improve rating quality through **mutual co-operation** among domestic CRAs by the Association of Credit Rating Agencies in Asia (ACRAA). However, the rating scales and processes vary across jurisdictions, posing challenges in objectivity, transparency and the quality of the analysis. Harmonisation of credit rating practices of CRAs in Asia in line with the IOSCO Code of Conduct Fundamentals for Credit Rating Agencies could help to achieve a degree of comparability across rating agencies in terms of rating methodology, rating criteria, definitions, benchmarks and overall rating process (IOSCO, 2015[9]).

Policy considerations:

- Ensure the existence of well-functioning diverse credit rating assessments for corporate bonds and other debt securities at affordable prices for companies all sizes.
- Ensure credit rating agencies provide markets with accurate, reliable and comparable opinions. Moreover, they should follow rigorous standards, use solid methodologies, disclose their methodologies and be independent from market actors.
- Support the establishment of domestic rating agencies to increase the availability of credit ratings assessment in markets where domestic rating agencies are not established or still developing.
- Consider creating an alternative credit rating system for growth companies to provide credit risk assessments to the market. In this respect, existing authorities with the technical capacities and access to relevant data could be responsible for implementing an alternative credit rating system.
- Consider introducing incentives specifically for growth companies, such as covering the full or partial cost of obtaining a credit rating to issue a corporate bond, until the corporate bond market reaches a certain level of development.
- Encourage active participation in regional initiatives aimed at harmonising and improving the quality of the credit rating practices of CRAs in Asia to be in line with IOSCO Code of Conduct Fundamentals for CRAs. Enhancing the quality of the credit rating practices, disclosures and communications can contribute to attracting a greater number of cross-border investors.

1.4. Improved secondary market liquidity

A liquid market ensures an efficient price formation process, improves investor confidence and contributes to the overall functioning of capital markets. Corporate bond markets are inherently illiquid when compared with stock markets. This lack of liquidity could undermine the attractiveness of corporate bonds for certain investors and discourage companies to issue them in the first place. In Asia, corporate bond markets are characterised by low secondary market liquidity. Importantly, low levels of liquidity have been identified as the most important barrier to issue corporate bonds by 17 out of the 19 regulators responding to the survey.

To enhance liquidity in the corporate bond markets, it is essential to address various factors, including the functions of stock exchanges, OTC markets and derivative markets, as well as the engagement of market makers. Additionally, crucial considerations relate to ensuring the affordability of research on companies, the accessibility of price information, evaluating the cost of trading and appropriate taxation arrangements.

To have meaningful trading in the secondary market, a certain level of activity in primary corporate bond markets is essential. Measures aimed at developing **marketplaces** for issuing and trading corporate bonds will, in turn, support the overall development of corporate bond markets and support the liquidity of bonds in the secondary market. Moreover, stock exchanges also play important role in increasing transparency and the availability of consistent and comparable data, which are vital components in ensuring liquid markets. Corporate bonds are primarily traded over-the-counter (OTC). Globally, and in Asia, there is an increasing number of OTC markets managed by stock exchanges. In Asia, as part of the efforts to advance marketplaces for corporate bonds, 16 jurisdictions already have a dedicated segment for corporate bonds on their stock exchange and 13 have OTC markets. However, the level of activity in the markets calls for further efforts.

Ensuring an effective price discovery mechanism in markets requires **price transparency** in trading activities. This transparency could not only support investor confidence but also could increase investor participation in the markets. Numerous exchanges in Asia provide their participants with both pre- and post-trade information for listed bonds. However, the availability of information is less pronounced for bonds traded over-the-counter and on alternative trading systems. Moreover, the fact that most corporate bonds do not trade daily, makes it challenging to accurately price these instruments, possibly discouraging some investors to participate in these markets. This **lack of accurate pricing** makes it difficult to value these securities in investors' balance sheets. In Asia, some jurisdictions have introduced systems to provide reference pricing or disseminate market prices to the market.

Corporate bond markets rely on a **limited number of dealers** to provide liquidity by maintaining an inventory of corporate bonds for intermediation. Over the past decade, there has been a substantial decrease in the corporate bond holdings of security brokers and dealers (Çelik, Demirtaş and Isaksson, 2020[8]). At the same time, large corporate bondholders such as pension funds and insurance corporations often adopt buy-and-hold investment strategies, reducing the market liquidity even further. Among the dealers, **market makers** play a crucial role in providing liquidity in corporate bond markets. In Asia, despite many jurisdictions have provisions regarding market makers in their legal and regulatory frameworks, the OECD Survey reveals market makers are not active.

The availability of **affordable research on companies** issuing corporate bonds could support the development of the market by filling the informational gap between companies and investors, and therefore encouraging investment and supporting informed trading. This is particularly important for growth companies as they often lack analyst coverage. To mitigate the information gaps between growth companies and investors, many jurisdictions have introduced measures to provide research coverage for growth companies.

Two additional factors that could influence corporate bond market trading are **the cost of trading and the tax treatment of corporate bonds** (see also Section 1.7). The trading fee levels, and, for example, capital gains tax rates should not discourage market participants from engaging in trading activities. Furthermore, the process of declaring and paying the related taxes should be simple.

The existence of well-functioning **derivative markets** allows investors to manage the risks associated with their investments, including corporate bonds, as well as supporting market liquidity (see also Section 1.6). This has been recognised in the results of the *Annual AsianBondsOnline Bond Market Liquidity Survey* that covers nine Asian jurisdictions.[2] According to the survey, hedging mechanisms appeared as one of the most important structural issues requiring improvement for the development of corporate bond markets (ADB, 2022[10]).

Policy considerations:

- Establish a dedicated segment on the stock exchange with less stringent requirements and/or making it only dedicated to qualified investors.
- Ensure a level of price transparency that promotes efficient price discovery in corporate bond markets.
- Consider introducing systems to provide reference pricing and/or ensuring dissemination of market prices to the market.
- Ensure a well-functioning market making mechanism to support secondary market liquidity in corporate bond markets.
- Consider establishing a mechanism that provides independent quantitative research on growth companies to market participants at no cost.
- Ensure that trading fees, the tax treatment of corporate bonds and their related procedures do not discourage participation in the corporate bond market.

1.5. Diversified investor base

The composition and diversity of the investor base play a critical role in shaping the dynamism and resilience of corporate bond markets. As corporate bond markets serve as channels for companies to access capital, the presence of a diversified investor base is essential for fostering liquidity, stability and overall market efficiency. In Asia, the lack of investors and their lack of interest were identified as significant barriers to the development of corporate bond markets by 14 and 15 regulators, respectively.

The investor base differs across jurisdictions and relates to the level of development of the domestic financial market. In most of the developed corporate bond markets, **traditional institutional investors** such as pension funds and insurance corporations are among the largest holders of corporate bonds. In these markets, pension reforms have contributed to their expansion, therefore, deepening the domestic institutional base for many types of financial products, including corporate bonds. While pension funds and insurance corporations are particularly well-suited for investment in corporate bonds with longer maturities due to the long-term structure of their liabilities, they typically invest in government bonds. The existence of regulatory requirements or self-imposed rules to manage the risks associated with their corporate bond investments limits the allocation of these investors to corporate bonds, often requiring a minimum credit rating for investments. Asian institutional investors are relatively large investors worldwide, as their assets represent a significant share of world's total assets of pension funds and insurance companies, therefore they have the potential to become important investors in regional capital markets.

Moreover, the presence of traditional institutional investors does not guarantee investments in **corporate bonds issued by growth companies**. These companies often face challenges in attracting institutional investors, as the nominal amounts are small and/or investors favour higher rated instruments. According to the OECD Survey, 19 jurisdictions permit bond issuances to domestic qualified investors.

The state of economic resilience, political stability and efficiency of the regulatory framework are necessary for a well-functioning corporate bond market, particularly to **attract foreign investors**. Capital controls, investment restrictions and the availability of risk mitigation instruments could also limit their participation in cross-border activities. Additionally, burdensome administrative requirements and procedures may discourage them to participate in corporate bond markets. In Asia, several jurisdictions have liberalised capital flows to improve foreign investor participation. Bond issuances to foreign qualified investors are allowed in all of the surveyed jurisdictions, with 15 allowing corporate bonds to be issued to non-domestic retail investors. However, some restrictions exist for these investors, particularly when it comes to growth-company bonds. Certain markets do not allow corporate bond issuances to any foreign investor, and others prevent growth companies from issuing corporate bonds to foreign investors. The development of the local asset management industry also offers an avenue to foreign investors to participate in domestic corporate bond markets.

Corporate bond markets are often not targeted to **retail investors**. Their participation, either directly or indirectly via collective investment vehicles, can significantly contribute to diversify the investor base. While several advanced markets have actively promoted increased participation of retail investors, the lack of financial knowledge may still impede their investment in corporate bonds. In the OECD Survey, the lack of financial knowledge and awareness of investors in the region has been identified as an important barrier for the development of corporate bond markets by 12 jurisdictions surveyed. This impedes investors' ability to assess the benefits and risks of corporate bond investments, thereby limiting the expansion of corporate bond markets.

Policy considerations:

- Assess the legal, regulatory and institutional framework governing institutional investors, taking into account its impact on the capital available to growth companies. Continue reforming the pension systems and supporting the development of insurance corporations in the region.
- Address regulatory obstacles, the cost of accessing the market and taxation issues for foreign investors.
- Promote the direct or indirect participation of retail investors while ensuring the risks taken by these investors are well understood and properly managed.
- Increase the financial literacy of retail investors. This could be done in collaboration with the private sector and stock exchanges by offering informative sessions to retail investors to raise awareness about the benefits and risks involved when participating in capital markets.

1.6. Instruments to attract a large pool of investors and diversify risk

Lower-rated, unrated or smaller issuers face impediments when they access or intend to access corporate bond markets, primarily due to the costs associated with issuing corporate bonds and higher interest rates demanded by investors. Moreover, in markets with a limited understanding of risk, investors tend to exhibit greater risk aversion towards lower-rated growth companies, as well as those in their early stages of development or with limited track records. To address these challenges the development of securitised instruments, the establishment of guarantee mechanisms and the availability of risk management instruments could present opportunities for these issuers to access corporate bond markets and also can provide investors with opportunities to diversify risks when investing in growth companies.

The **securitisation** enables the pooling of a group of debt instruments issued by smaller issuers, creating a larger security-backed instrument issued by a special purpose vehicle (SPV). Typically, through this process companies' idiosyncratic risks can be somewhat diversified. In addition, guarantees can also be used to enhance the credit quality of issuers allowing companies to pay a lower risk premium. Furthermore, by pooling smaller issuances into a large-securitised bond, makes the instrument more attractive to large investors. Notably, Korea has implemented a securitisation mechanism, in the form of collateralised debt obligations, enabling SMEs to collectively issue corporate bonds. Meanwhile, bonds issued via Italy's mini-bond framework are also securitised into basket bonds in some cases, where bond portfolios from a group of companies are transformed into a consolidated pool of securities and then issued by an SPV. In addition to securitisation, the use of **guarantees** could enhance the risk profile of some issuers. Guarantees reduce a company's risk and increase investors' appetite for these instruments.

The existence of **well-functioning derivative markets** is crucial for enabling investors to effectively manage the risks associated with their investments, including corporate bonds, and to enhance market liquidity. Derivative markets have the potential to draw foreign investors to local currency corporate bonds by providing them with the means to hedge against the currency risks associated with their investments. Simultaneously, instruments like interest rate derivatives and credit default swaps (CDS) could help investors mitigate fluctuations in interest rates and manage default risks on their corporate bonds investment. Fourteen jurisdictions have a functioning derivative market to help manage risks associated with corporate bond investments. Both financial instruments for mitigating currency risk and interest rate risk are offered in 12 jurisdictions, while CDS are available in only eight jurisdictions. However, most of these markets have a limited number of participants and therefore limited activity.

Another practice in terms of risk diversification when investing in growth-company bonds is to only allow **qualified investors**[3] to invest in this market. This ensures that only investors who have the financial sophistication and capacity to understand and manage the associated risks are participating in more complex or higher-risk investments. For example, in the mini-bond framework of Italy, SMEs can issue corporate bonds without a rating, however only qualified investors are allowed to invest in these bonds.

Policy considerations:

- Introduce a securitisation mechanism to promote the development of corporate bond markets for growth companies.
- Establish a guarantee scheme to support growth companies' access to market-based financing.
- Continue developing the derivative markets to provide risk management tools to investors and intermediaries investing in corporate bonds.
- Develop corporate bond markets for growth companies to qualified investors first until the market reaches a certain size and is more developed.

1.7. Role of government and other initiatives

Well-functioning capital markets can support sustainable economic growth by channelling resources to the corporate sector and by offering saving tools to households. Often governments incorporate capital market development and the diversification of funding sources for growth companies into their reform agendas including. As part of these reform agendas, one of the initiatives is improving the government bond market. Moreover, within their capacity, governments could make use of fiscal tools, introduce task forces, establish private-public initiatives and launch campaigns. Recognising the crucial role of collaboration in developing bond markets, authorities could also participate in regional initiatives.

Among the tools available to authorities, **taxation** could play a crucial role in the development of corporate bond markets. The tax treatment of corporate bonds can impact their overall attractiveness and cost-effectiveness. Excessive or disproportionate taxes can discourage companies from issuing corporate bonds and investors from investing in them. Governments often design tax policies that aim to strike a balance between encouraging capital market activity and ensuring the principles of sound fiscal management. According to the results of the OECD Survey, corporate bonds are taxed similarly in structure in the region with differences in the rates and conditions applied (see Section 3.4 in Chapter 3).

Appropriately designed **tax incentives or exemptions** could facilitate the development of corporate bond markets allowing a significant number of companies to access market-based financing therefore reducing their dependence on bank loans. Only a few jurisdictions in the region use tax credits and exemptions to encourage the use of corporate bonds. However, while these incentives and exemptions target all types of issuers, there is currently no specific tax incentive directly targeted at bond issuances by growth companies.

Corporate bond issuance involves many **costs** such as expenses related to preparing a prospectus, complying with new disclosure requirements, attaining a credit rating and direct issuance costs. These direct issuance costs cover regulatory fees, legal fees, underwriter fees and, if the bond is intended to be listed, listing fees. These direct and indirect listing costs typically impose a heavier burden on growth companies, often discouraging them from issuing corporate bonds.

An important example of supporting the use of corporate bonds by growth companies outside of Asia is the **mini-bond framework in Italy**. Authorities created a special framework that enables unlisted SMEs to issue bonds with less strict requirements, such as without a rating and with a less costly issuance process compared to traditional bonds. Issuers can also list their mini-bonds on a dedicated segment of the stock exchange reserved only for qualified investors. Additionally, mini-bonds come with tax advantages, which enhances their appeal as a financing option for companies and as investment option for investors. Notably, mini-bonds have also been securitised through SPVs, to create a diversified pool of companies available for institutional investors.

Stock exchanges globally are establishing **dedicated segments** tailored to meet the needs of growth companies. These segments, provide a platform for growth companies to access public funding, raise capital and enhance their visibility. Exchanges typically streamline the listing requirements for these segments, making them more accessible to smaller companies. The goal is to encourage entrepreneurship, support innovation and diversify investment opportunities.

Industry-led bodies or associations can play a valuable role in promoting the development of corporate bond markets, lifting the standards of the industry, improving the products offered to investors and creating a corporate bond market landscape that support bondholder rights. In eleven of the surveyed jurisdictions, there is an industry-led body or industry association that is active in relation to the corporate bond market. The role of these associations varies across jurisdictions from having a self-regulatory role in some of them to promoting and developing the debt securities market in others.

Regional efforts to develop bond markets could contribute to and amplify initiatives at the country level. Importantly, they could foster financial integration, encourage cross-border investment and enhance the resilience of interconnected markets. The Asian Bond Markets Initiative (ABMI) has a main objective to strengthen and develop local currency bond markets in the region. Additionally, the Asia Securities Industry and Financial Markets Association (ASIFMA) plays an important role in promoting the development of bond markets in the region and internationally, sharing best practices and leveraging international experiences. ASIFMA has launched initiatives on critical issues such as bond issuance, credit ratings, transparency and electronification, tax and compliance.

Companies, in particular growth companies, also may lack **financial knowledge** about the benefits of corporate bonds and the **technical capacity** to use market-based financing in general. Therefore, financial education of company management is important, particularly in markets where the capital market development is in its early stage.

Policy considerations:

- Establish a comprehensive reform agenda to promote growth companies' access to corporate bond markets. This agenda could include various steps and clearly define the responsibilities of relevant authorities with a focus on growth companies' access to corporate bond markets. This can be achieved by creating a task force, committee or a public-private programme that ensures regular follow-up on the implementation of identified measures.
- Review the taxation framework to support growth companies' access to financing and simplify tax declaration and payment procedures. Implementing tax incentives, such as the elimination or reduction of taxes and offering tax credits, could be beneficial for the market development, but have to be balanced with broader economic considerations. These incentives could be designed to be in place for a certain period of time and could target only certain segments of the market such as bonds issued by growth companies.
- Establish a dedicated segment for growth companies on the stock exchange using proportional listing requirements and less stringent rules, while ensuring appropriate investor protection.
- Enhance the role of industry-led bodies or associations in corporate bond markets. Reforms could include the creation of such bodies or associations and support these entities to develop corporate bond markets. This could involve, for example, developing a template for corporate bond terms, advocating for the better protection of bondholder rights and promoting good practices among market participants.
- Establish targeted financial education or awareness campaigns to inform corporate executives and other relevant actors about the opportunities of corporate bond financing.

References

ADB (2022), *Asia Small and Medium-sized Enterprise Monitor 2022*, https://doi.org/10.22617/SGP220540-2. [1]

ADB (2022), *AsianBondsOnline Annual Bond Market Liquidity Survey*, https://asianbondsonline.adb.org/documents/abm/abm_mar_2022_abo_annual_bond_market_liquidity_survey.pdf. [10]

Çelik, S., G. Demirtaş and M. Isaksson (2020), *Corporate Bond Market Trends, Emerging Risks and Monetary Policy*, OECD, Paris, https://www.oecd.org/corporate/Corporate-Bond-Market-Trends-Emerging-Risks-and-Monetary-Policy.htm. [8]

Gambacorta, L., J. Yang and K. Tsatsaronis (2014), "Financial structure and growth", *BIS Quarterly Review*, https://www.bis.org/publ/qtrpdf/r_qt1403e.htm. [3]

IOSCO (2015), "IOSCO Code of Conduct Fundamentals for Credit Rating Agencies", https://www.iosco.org/library/pubdocs/pdf/IOSCOPD482.pdf. [9]

OECD (2023), *G20/OECD Principles of Corporate Governance 2023*, OECD Publishing, Paris, https://doi.org/10.1787/ed750b30-en. [6]

OECD (2023), "OECD Code of Liberalisation of Capital Movements", OECD, Paris, https://www.oecd.org/investment/codes.htm. [5]

OECD (2022), *Corporate Finance in Asia and the COVID-19 Crisis*, OECD, Paris, https://www.oecd.org/publications/corporate-finance-in-asia-and-the-covid-19-crisis-87861cf0-en.htm. [4]

World Bank (2014), *Debt Resolution and Business Exit: Insolvency Reform for Credit, Entrepreneurship, and Growth*, https://documents.worldbank.org/en/publication/documents-reports/documentdetail/912041468178733220/debt-resolution-and-business-exit-insolvency-reform-for-credit-entrepreneurship-and-growth. [7]

Yoshino, N. and F. Taghizadeh-Hesary (2018), *The Role of SMEs in Asia and Their Difficulties in Accessing Finance*, https://www.adb.org/sites/default/files/publication/474576/adbi-wp911.pdf. [2]

Notes

[1] Australia, India, Indonesia, Singapore.

[2] China, Hong Kong (China), Indonesia, Korea, Malaysia, Philippines, Singapore, Thailand and Viet Nam.

[3] Qualified investors refer to individuals or institutions that meet specific regulatory criteria allowing them to participate in certain financial activities or investments that are not readily available to the general public.

2 Corporate bond markets activity in Asia

This chapter provides an overview of the use of market- and bank-based financing by Asian non-financial companies. It then provides trends in the use of corporate bonds in Asia and compares it with global trends. Furthermore, it shows trends in the use of corporate bonds by growth companies in the region and globally, focusing on their maturity, industry composition and credit quality.

2.1. Market-based financing in Asia

In recent years, Asia has seen a rapid advancement in both corporate bond and public equity markets. As depicted in Figure 2.1, non-financial Asian companies have around USD 4 trillion in outstanding corporate bonds, equivalent to 11% of the region's GDP. At the same time, Asian listed non-financial companies have a combined market capitalisation of USD 26 trillion, equivalent to 75% of GDP. However, significant differences exist among economies in the region. While the People's Republic of China (hereafter 'China') leads in sheer volume for both non-financial corporate bonds and market capitalisation of listed non-financial companies, its ratios to GDP remain relatively modest compared to jurisdictions like Japan and Korea. Focusing on corporate bonds, financial hubs such as Hong Kong (China) are noteworthy. Moreover, countries like Thailand, Korea and Japan stand out as their outstanding non-financial corporate bonds represent 21%, 19% and 15% of their GDP, respectively.

Figure 2.1. Overview of non-financial companies' access to market-based financing and bank-credit, 2022

	Outstanding corporate bonds		Listed companies		Bank credit	
	Amount (USD billions)	% of GDP	Market cap. (USD billions)	% of GDP	Amount (USD billions)	% of GDP
By region						
Global	15 400	15%	83 809	84%	86 790	96%
Asia	4 123	11%	26 170	75%	49 744	143%
By jurisdiction						
Hong Kong (China)	93	26%	2 891	// 801%	952	// 264%
Thailand	110	21%	484	90%	649	121%
Korea	312	19%	1 502	90%	2 914	175%
Japan	652	15%	4 811	114%	5 158	122%
China	2430	13%	10 106	56%	33 551	185%
Chinese Taipei	77	10%	1 250	// 164%	Not available	Not available
Singapore	47	10%	271	58%	603	129%
Australia	161	9%	1 218	72%	2 278	134%
Philippines	32	8%	192	48%	197	49%
Indonesia	62	5%	394	30%	403	31%
India	135	4%	2 588	76%	1 788	53%
Mongolia	0.4	3%	1	6%	7	41%
Malaysia	9	2%	287	70%	462	113%
Viet Nam	2	0.6%	112	28%	514	126%
Sri Lanka	0.2	0.3%	8	11%	35	47%
Pakistan	1	0.1%	23	6%	56	15%
Bangladesh	0.1	0.01%	32	7%	179	39%

Note: In this figure, "Asia" refers to the jurisdictions that participated in the OECD Survey, including 18 Asian jurisdictions and Australia.
Source: OECD Capital Market Series dataset, Bank for International Settlements, World Bank, LSEG.

Asian markets exhibit a pronounced dependence on bank financing. In Asia, bank credit extended to non-financial companies stands at 143% of GDP, much higher than the global number at 96% (Figure 2.1). Moreover, there are significant differences across economies. For instance, Hong Kong (China) and China have bank credit to non-financial corporations to GDP ratios at 264% and 185%, respectively. Additionally, Korea's bank credit to non-financial corporations makes up over 175% of GDP. In Australia, Japan, Singapore, Thailand and Viet Nam, bank credit to non-financial corporations represents around 120% of GDP.

In the majority of Asian jurisdictions, market-based financing plays a secondary role compared to bank-based financing. Figure 2.2 shows the relationship between market-based financing and bank-based financing. Market-based financing is defined as the sum of the market capitalisation of non-financial listed companies and the outstanding amount of non-financial corporate bonds. Notably, despite the rapid development of both public equity and corporate bond markets in some Asian markets, corporations still rely heavily on bank financing. For example, market-based financing in China accounted for 69% of GDP in 2022, significantly less than bank credit which accounted for 185% of GDP. In Viet Nam, the scenario is even more pronounced: bank-based financing represents a substantial 126% of GDP, more than four times the contribution of market-based financing, which is just under 30%. Importantly, it is only in a few jurisdictions that market-based financing exceeds bank-based financing. In Japan, for example, both types of financing are highly developed. Non-financial companies' capital sourced from public equity and corporate bond markets together accounts for almost 130% of GDP, a Figure slightly higher than the 122% attributed to bank-based financing. Meanwhile, in India, bank-based financing represents slightly over 50% of GDP, much lower than the contribution from market-based financing (80%).

Figure 2.2. Market-based versus bank-based financing in non-financial companies in Asia, 2022

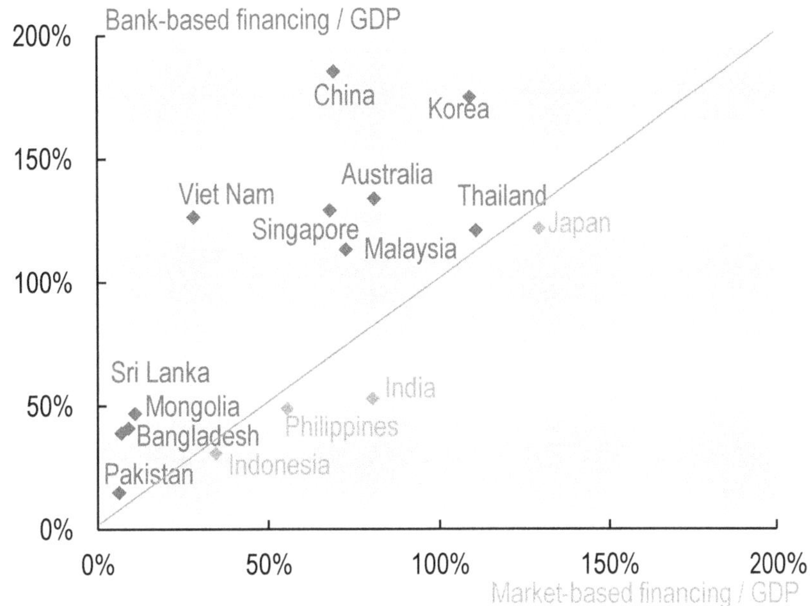

Note: Market-based financing is defined as the sum of the market capitalisation of non-financial listed companies and the outstanding amount of non-financial corporate bonds. Bank-based financing is defined as bank credit to non-financial corporations.
Note: Hong Kong (China) is not shown on the graph since its values fall outside the limits of the graph with the market-based financing to GDP is 827% and bank-based financing to GDP is 264% of GDP.
Source: OECD Capital Market Series dataset, Bank for International Settlements, World Bank, LSEG.

2.2. The use of corporate bond markets by non-financial companies

Corporate bonds offer companies a way to diversify their financing sources and to access long-term financing. Since the global financial crisis, there has been a considerable increase in the use of corporate bonds by non-financial companies. Indeed, the global amount issued doubled from an annual average of USD 1 trillion before the global financial crisis (2000-07) to an annual average of more than USD 2 trillion in the period between 2008 and 2022. Globally, with the increasing use of corporate bonds, the outstanding amount of non-financial corporate bonds doubled from USD 7.7 trillion in 2008 to USD 15.4 trillion in 2022.

Following the outbreak of the COVID-19 crisis, corporate bonds served as an important source of financing for the non-financial corporate sector. In 2020 and 2021, global bond issuances by non-financial companies reached historical peaks of USD 3.3 trillion and USD 2.7 trillion, respectively. In 2022, in line with the tightening monetary policy, global bond issuance contracted by 36% with respect to the previous year and the volume issued by non-financial companies stood at USD 1.7 trillion.

Bond issuance in Asian markets has also significantly increased over the past two decades. The annual amount issued has grown from a relatively low level of USD 144 billion between 2000 and 2007 to USD 657 billion between 2008 and 2022. Annual capital raised via corporate bonds reached its peak (USD 1 trillion) in 2021, before contracting to USD 837 billion in 2022 following global trends (Figure 2.3, Panel A). Additionally, the outstanding amount of non-financial corporate bonds in the region reached USD 4.1 trillion in 2022 — more than four times the outstanding amount recorded in 2008 (Figure 2.3, Panel B). The Chinese corporate bond market has been the engine of this regional growth.

In line with the increasing use of corporate bonds by non-financial companies in Asia, the share of Asia in global corporate bond issuances and outstanding amounts increased significantly since 2000 (Figure 2.3, Panel C). In 2000, Asia's non-financial corporate bond issuance represented only 16% of global issuance, whereas by 2022, Asian non-financial corporations issued half of the global amount. Similarly, Asia's share in global outstanding amounts of corporate bonds increased from 17% in 2000, to 27% in 2022.

Figure 2.3. Asian non-financial corporate bonds

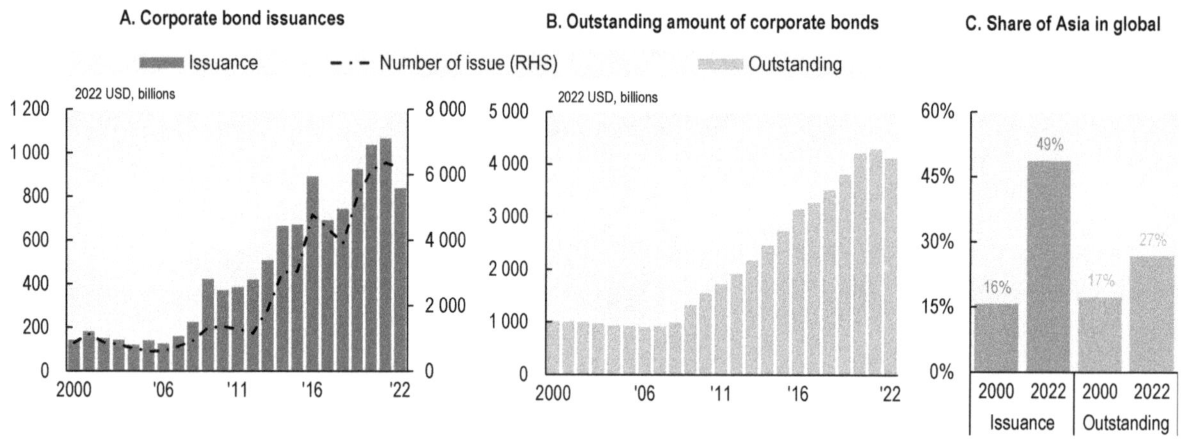

Note: In this figure, "Asia" refers to the jurisdictions that participated in the OECD Survey, including 18 Asian jurisdictions and Australia.
Source: OECD Capital Market Series Dataset, LSEG, see Annex B for details.

2.3. The use of corporate bond markets by non-financial growth companies

Over the past two decades, corporate bond markets have also been offering financing opportunities for smaller companies, particularly in Asia. An increasing number of growth companies have raised capital from regional corporate bond markets. Growth company bonds in this chapter are defined as issuances of less than USD 50 million.

The issuance by growth companies doubled in the period following the global financial crisis compared to the pre-global financial crisis period, from an annual average of USD 9.6 billion to USD 18.4 billion. Still, in 2022, the amount of corporate bond issued by non-financial growth companies only represented a very small share (2%) of global issuances, while representing one-fourth of the total number of corporate bond issuances. Notably, in the wake of the COVID-19 crisis, growth companies tapped corporate bond markets, increasing the volume issued by 32% compared to 2019 – the largest annual increase observed in the past two decades. In 2022, while global bond issuance contracted significantly, non-financial growth companies continued using this market, raising USD 39 billion. Globally, outstanding amounts of non-financial corporate bonds by growth companies stood at USD 121 billion in 2022.

Bond issuance by Asian growth companies has also increased significantly, particularly following the global financial crisis. The annual amount issued grew from USD 5.7 billion in 2000 to USD 33.3 billion in 2022 (Figure 2.4, Panel A). The non-financial growth-company bonds represented 4% of all corporate bond issuances in Asia in 2022 and 27% of the total number of bonds — higher than the growth-company bonds' share in global numbers. Additionally, the outstanding amount of these bonds in the region was USD 90.5 billion in 2022 (Figure 2.4, Panel B). Chinese and Korean companies have been driving the observed growth in this market. Overall, the Asian growth-company bond market dominates at the global level (Figure 2.4, Panel C). In 2000, Asian non-financial growth-company bonds represented 44% of the global amount issued by non-financial growth companies whereas in 2022 this was 85%. Similarly, Asia's share in global outstanding amounts increased from being 24% in 2000, to 75% in 2022.

Figure 2.4. Asian non-financial growth-company bonds

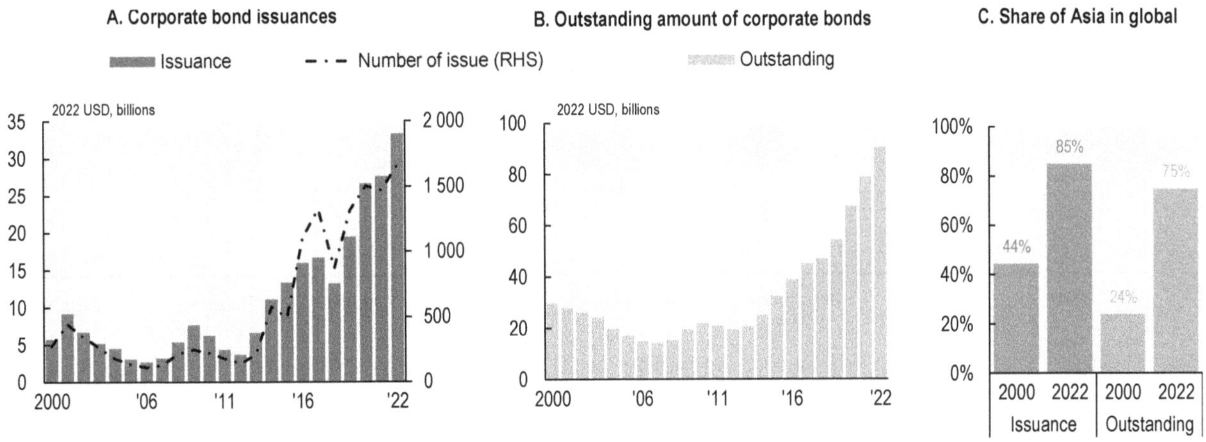

Note: In this figure, "Asia" refers to the jurisdictions that participated in the OECD Survey, including 18 Asian jurisdictions and Australia.
Source: OECD Capital Market Series Dataset, LSEG, see Annex B for details.

In almost all Asian jurisdictions, except Japan and Singapore, corporate bond markets for growth companies have expanded since 2000 (Figure 2.5). While in Japan, the amounts issued between the 2000-11 and 2012-22 periods were similar, in Singapore, the overall amount issued in the second period contracted by 60%. China shows the largest expansion with an almost non-existent growth-company bond market in the 2000-11 period to issuing USD 68.3 billion during the latest period. In the 2012-22 period, Korea ranked first with the highest amount of growth-company bonds (USD 68.7 billion), followed by China, Thailand and India.

In line with the issuance trends, Korea and China had the highest amount of outstanding growth-company bonds in 2022 (Figure 2.6). Indeed, Korea and China together made up 74% of the Asian outstanding amounts in 2022, recording USD 34.4 billion and USD 32.2 billion, respectively. Thailand, India and Japan followed with outstanding amounts of around USD 4 billion, while the remaining jurisdictions had outstanding amounts of growth-company bonds below USD 3 billion.

Figure 2.5. Issuance of Asian non-financial growth-company bonds by jurisdictions

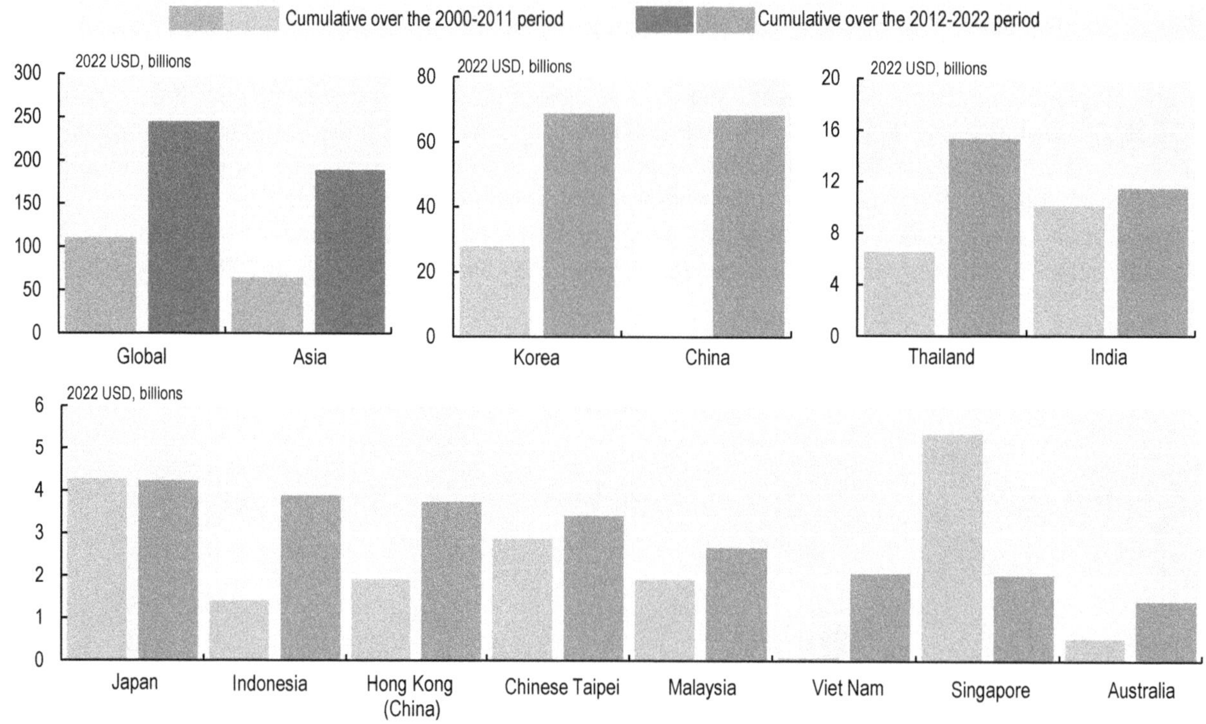

Note: In this figure, "Asia" refers to the jurisdictions that participated in the OECD Survey, including 18 Asian jurisdictions and Australia.
Note: There is no information on growth companies' corporate bond issuances from Bangladesh, Cambodia, Mongolia and Sri Lanka, and the amounts are too small for Lao PDR and Philippines. Therefore, these jurisdictions are excluded from the figure.
Source: OECD Capital Market Series Dataset, LSEG, see Annex B for details.

Figure 2.6. Outstanding amounts of Asian non-financial growth-company bonds, 2022

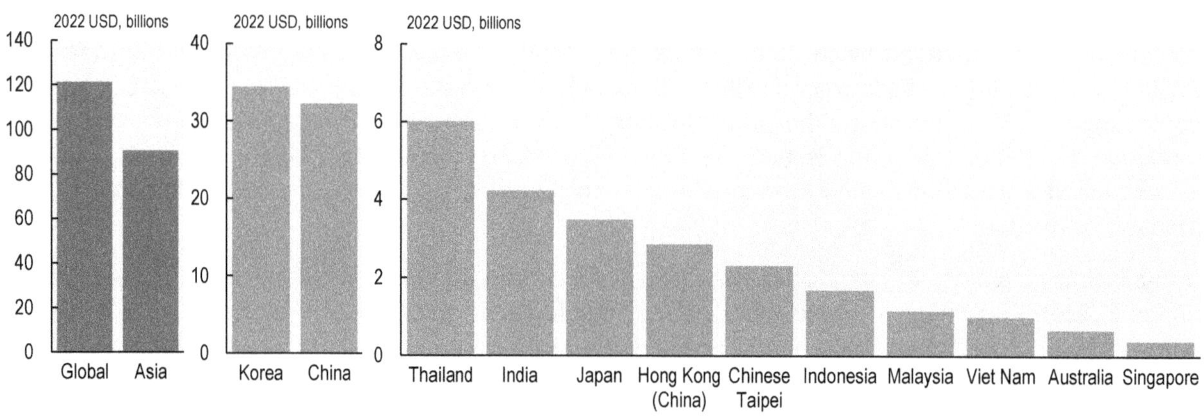

Note: In this figure, "Asia" refers to the jurisdictions that participated in the OECD Survey, including 18 Asian jurisdictions and Australia.
Note: There is no information on growth companies' corporate bond issuances from Bangladesh, Cambodia, Mongolia and Sri Lanka, and the amounts are too small for Lao PDR, Pakistan and Philippines. Therefore, these jurisdictions are excluded from the figure.
Source: OECD Capital Market Series Dataset, LSEG, see Annex B for details.

Growth-company bonds typically have shorter maturities compared to those issued by larger companies. This difference is mostly influenced by the risk profile of these companies. Investors perceive growth companies as riskier due to uncertainties associated with their evolving business models and market positions. Consequently, they tend to demand higher interest rates for longer maturities to compensate the additional perceived risk. As a result, growth companies often opt for shorter-maturity bonds to secure financing more feasibly.

Globally, while large-company bonds have an average maturity of 9 years, growth-company bonds have a much shorter average tenor of just 4.4 years (Figure 2.7). In Asia, the maturity gap between large- and growth-company bonds is narrower than the one observed at the global level. Growth-company bonds have an average maturity of 4.2 years, only 1.2 years shorter compared to large-company bonds. India, Singapore and Hong Kong (China) exhibit the largest gap in maturity between large- and growth-company bonds, with growth-company bonds issued in 2022 maturing about 6 years before than those issued by large companies. Interestingly, in Australia and Viet Nam, corporate bonds issued by growth companies (driven by few issuances) have longer maturities than those issued by large firms. Korea has one of the largest markets for growth-company bonds allowing growth companies to borrow at maturities comparable to large companies.

Figure 2.7. Average maturities of Asian non-financial large- and growth-company bonds, 2022

	A. Growth companies (Years)	B. Large companies (Years)	C. Maturity gap (large - growth) (Years)
Global	4.4	9.0	4.6
Asia	4.2	5.4	1.2
Australia	12.9	8.4	-4.5
Japan	8.3	10.2	1.9
Korea	5.4	5.2	-0.2
Viet Nam	4.6	3.8	-0.7
Chinese Taipei	4.4	7.8	3.4
India	3.8	10.4	6.6
Indonesia	3.5	7.3	3.8
Malaysia	3.5	4.2	0.7
Singapore	3.1	10.1	7.0
China	3.0	4.2	1.2
Thailand	2.9	5.6	2.7
Hong Kong (China)	2.6	9.5	6.9

Note: In this figure, "Asia" refers to the jurisdictions that participated in the OECD Survey, including 18 Asian jurisdictions and Australia.
Note: There is no information on growth companies' corporate bond issuances from Bangladesh, Cambodia, Mongolia and Sri Lanka, and the amounts are too small for Lao PDR, Pakistan and Philippines. Therefore, these jurisdictions are excluded from the figures.
Source: OECD Capital Market Series Dataset, LSEG, see Annex B for details.

The industry distribution of corporate bond issuances by Asian growth companies largely mirrored that of large companies over the 2000-22 period. The industrials sector alone accounted for more than half of the total issuances from growth companies, followed by cyclical consumers and utilities (Figure 2.8, Panel A). Across markets, there are also some differences. In almost all jurisdictions, the industrials sector dominates the issuance of growth-company bonds. The exceptions are Australia and Viet Nam, where non-cyclical consumer and cyclical consumer sectors, respectively, take the lead. Furthermore, growth companies from the cyclical consumer sector represent a significant share of issuance across Asian markets, accounting for 53% in Viet Nam and over a quarter in both Singapore and Malaysia. The utilities sector constitutes 30% of growth company proceeds in Hong Kong (China), and over 10% in Australia, Japan, India and Thailand (Figure 2.8, Panel B).

Figure 2.8. Industry distribution of Asian non-financial growth-company bonds, 2000-22

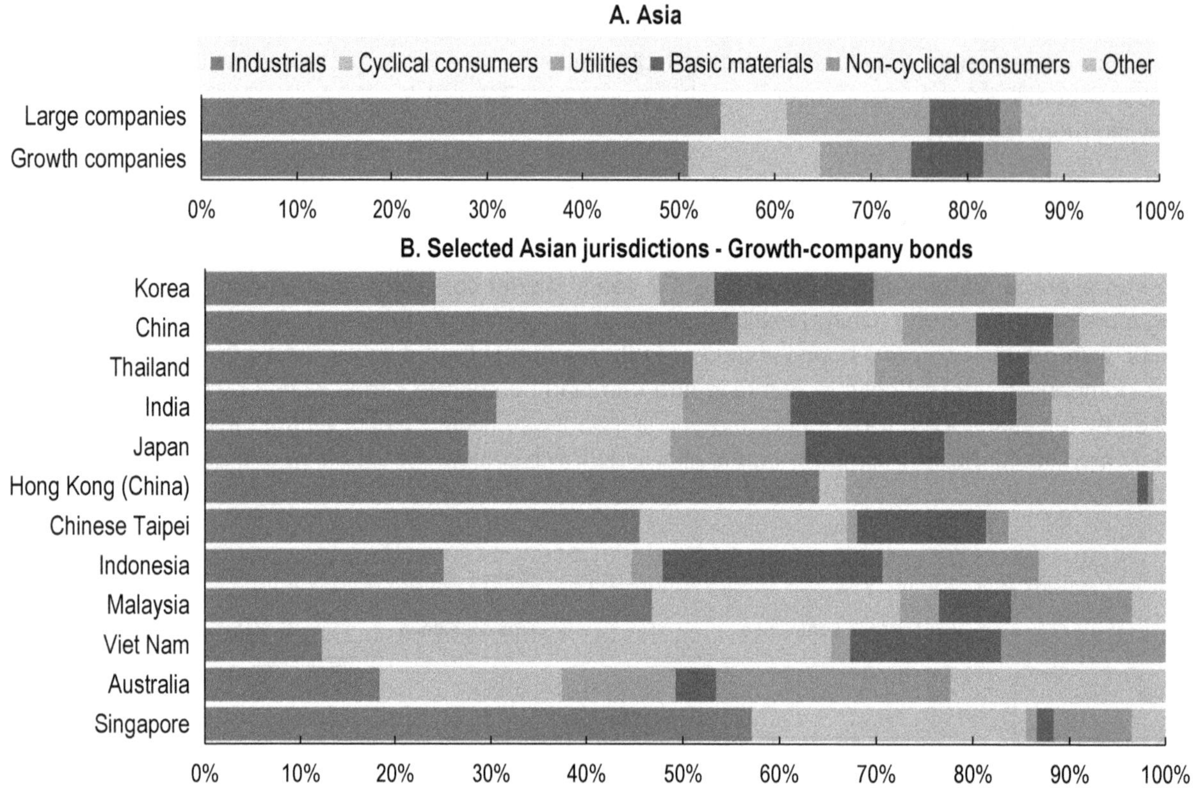

Note: In this figure, "Asia" refers to the jurisdictions that participated in the OECD Survey, including 18 Asian jurisdictions and Australia.
Note: The industry distribution is computed by calculating the cumulative amount issued by industry between 2000 and 2022 in each jurisdiction/region. There is no information on growth-company bond issuances from Bangladesh, Cambodia, Mongolia and Sri Lanka, and the amounts are too small for Lao PDR, Pakistan and Philippines. Therefore, these jurisdictions are excluded from the figure. The "Other" category includes energy, healthcare, technology and telecommunication services.
Source: OECD Capital Market Series Dataset, LSEG, see Annex B for details.

While there has been a global surge in non-investment grade corporate bonds, growth companies have not contributed much to this trend. Globally, the annual issuance of non-investment grade corporate bonds represented on average 18% of total issuance between 2000 and 2022. In Asia, this share was significantly lower with only 4% of total annual issuance corresponding to non-investment grade bonds. Non-investment grade corporate bond issued by growth companies only represented an average share in total proceeds of 0.1% globally and 0.4% in Asia (Figure 2.9).

Figure 2.9. Non-investment grade corporate bonds by non-financial growth companies, average share in total issuance 2000-22

Note: In this figure, "Asia" refers to the jurisdictions that participated in the OECD Survey, including 18 Asian jurisdictions and Australia. Data refers to the annual average share of non-investment grade bonds issued by non-financial growth companies in total issuance.
Source: OECD Capital Market Series Dataset, LSEG, see Annex B for details.

3 General information on corporate bond markets in Asia

This chapter provides an overview of corporate bond markets, covering the procedures to issue a corporate bond, measures supporting access to these markets, the perceived barriers to the development of corporate bond markets and the tax treatment of corporate bonds. It derives insights from the OECD survey conducted among 19 regulators from 18 Asian jurisdictions and Australia.

3.1. General information on corporate bond markets

While there are some common aspects the bond issuance process and, importantly, the procedures for growth companies to access corporate bond markets vary across jurisdictions in Asia. To better understand the current corporate bond market landscape, the OECD conducted a comprehensive survey targeted to regulators, the *OECD Survey on Access to Corporate Bond Markets for Growth Companies in Asia* (hereafter "OECD Survey"). Regulators from 18 Asian jurisdictions and Australia[1] provided responses. Among other things, the OECD Survey examines issues such as the corporate bond issuance procedure, measures to support corporate access to corporate bond markets, tax treatment of corporate bonds, barriers to the development of corporate bond markets, marketplaces for issuing and trading corporate bonds, credit rating requirements and bondholder rights.

When analysing the main requirements for issuing corporate bonds, the OECD Survey shows that **the three most common are the submission of a prospectus, the existence of historical financial statements, and the periodic and ongoing disclosure of key information** (Figure 3.1).[2] The prospectus is a vital information source for investors about the securities that companies are issuing and about the company itself. As discussed later in this chapter, in certain cases the issuance process for corporate bonds exempts companies from issuing a prospectus or permits the submission of a simplified prospectus. Historical financial statements are also highlighted as necessary documents for the issuance to take place as they normally provide outsiders critical information about the issuer's financial position.

In 14 of the surveyed jurisdictions, the issuer needs to have a certain legal form to be able to issue a corporate bond. In Malaysia, the entities authorised to issue bonds primarily include listed companies, licensed banks and some public institutions. If an unlisted company wishes to issue corporate bonds, it must be guaranteed by another eligible entity (SC Malaysia, 2021[1]). Similarly, Lao PDR only permits corporate bond issuance by public companies and limited companies (Lao Securities Commission, 2014[2]). In Thailand, issuers of corporate bonds are not limited to listed companies, but the fast-track approval process is available for these companies only (ADB, 2021[3]).

Registration with the regulatory authority to issue a corporate bond is mandatory in 13 of the surveyed jurisdictions. Malaysia, for instance, requires an application letter which includes, among many other things, information on ultimate shareholders, profile of board members of the issuing company and sources of repayment (SC Malaysia, 2021[1]). Philippines requires the submission of a registration statement, which includes issuers information and brief descriptive information in the prospectus (ADB, 2017[4]). The Indonesian regulatory authority provides a template for registration. The template requires details to be provided about the activities of underwriters and selling agents at primary markets, and regional and ownership dispersion of the issuer (ADB, 2021[5]). Bangladesh, India, Malaysia and Sri Lanka do not require registration with the authority.

Approval by the regulatory authority to issue a corporate bond is mandatory in 12 jurisdictions. Obtaining approval is generally considered more stringent than registering with the authority, leading to a differentiated framework for corporate bond issuances based on their characteristics, including target investors. In Korea, the Financial Services Commission (FSC) requires its approval for corporate bonds offered to the public while debt securities traded on the stock exchange are exempt from this, provided that they meet listing requirements (ADB, 2018[6]). Despite the absence of registration with the regulatory authority, corporate bond issuers in Bangladesh and Malaysia still need to submit the relevant documents for approval by the authority (SC Malaysia, 2022[7]).

In seven jurisdictions (Cambodia, Chinese Taipei, Indonesia, Lao PDR, Mongolia, Pakistan, Philippines, Thailand and Viet Nam) both registration and approval are mandatory. In India, where corporate bonds are neither required to registered nor approved by the regulatory authority, issuers are required to list their bonds on the stock exchange, which therefore ensures that the assessment of the issuers' eligibility is done by the stock exchange (SEBI, 2019[8]).

Nine jurisdictions impose quantitative requirements to issue corporate bonds such as a minimum amount of the corporate bond issuance or a limitation of the issuance. As an example of a minimum amount requirement of the issuance, Chinese Taipei requires issuers for overseas securities to issue at least USD 20 million. In Lao PDR, listing requirements when issuing bonds to the public include a minimum amount of at least LAK 3 billion (c. USD 145 000) (Lao Securities Exchange, 2011[9]). On the contrary, four jurisdictions (China, Chinese Taipei, Mongolia and Viet Nam) set limitations on corporate bond issuance. Chinese Taipei and Viet Nam impose limitations on bonds issued by foreign issuers while Mongolia does not allow the value of the debt instrument to surpass the company's equity capital.

Figure 3.1. The main requirements for a non-financial company to issue corporate bonds

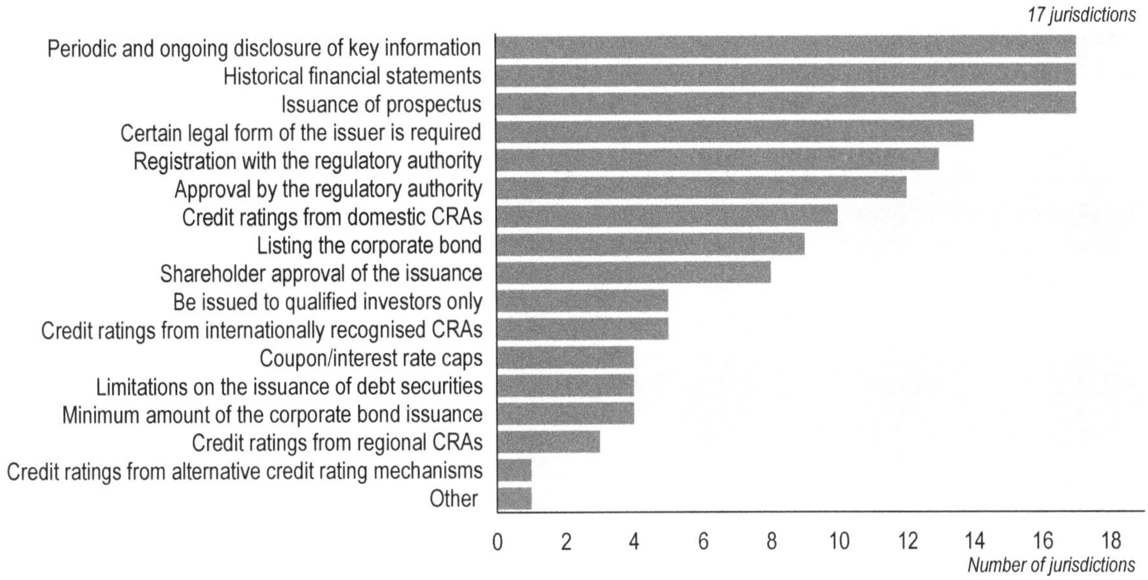

Source: OECD Survey on Access to Corporate Bond Markets for Growth Companies in Asia, see Annex B for details.

Credit ratings are required to issue a corporate bond in 11 jurisdictions. Credit ratings from domestic agencies are mentioned as one of the main requirements by 10 jurisdictions, followed by ratings from internationally recognised CRAs by 5 jurisdictions and regional CRAs by 3 jurisdictions. Cambodia, India and Lao PDR accept credit ratings from any type of credit rating agency. Interestingly, Lao PDR accepts credit ratings from alternative credit rating mechanisms (see details in Chapter 5).

Corporate bonds must be listed in nine jurisdictions (Bangladesh, Cambodia, China, Indonesia, Lao PDR, Mongolia, Pakistan, Philippines and Chinese Taipei). In terms of listing requirements, minimum issuance size requirements are set in Cambodia and Philippines, at KHR 1 billion and PHP 100 million respectively. Additional listing requirements include a minimum number of years in operation (Indonesia and Mongolia), a record of certain positive profits (Indonesia, Lao PDR, and Mongolia) and the submission of audited financial statements (Bangladesh, Indonesia, and Mongolia). Among these jurisdictions, Bangladesh, Indonesia and Philippines require credit ratings from a rating agency authorised by the stock exchange or the regulator. Specifically, the Indonesia Stock Exchange requires an investment grade rating for corporate bonds seeking listing. It should be noted that obtaining a credit rating is not a mandatory requirement for issuing bonds in all jurisdictions (ADB, 2017[10]; Cambodia Securities Exchange, 2017[11]; Dhaka Stock Exchange, 2015[12]; Lao Securities Exchange, 2023[13]; Mongolian Stock Exchange, 2018[14]).

Shareholders' approval for issuing a corporate bond is required in eight jurisdictions and in certain jurisdictions (Korea, Malaysia, Mongolia, Sri Lanka and Chinese Taipei) corporate bonds can be issued only to qualified investors.

Six jurisdictions (Korea, Lao PDR, Mongolia, Pakistan, Thailand and Viet Nam) **offer standardised templates for corporate bond contracts** (Figure 3.2, Panel A). Providing a standardised template for corporate bond contracts, in particular for growth companies, could give companies clear guidance on the type of information needed to issue corporate bonds, therefore, facilitating the issuance procedure. These templates are provided by government authorities in Lao PDR, Thailand and Viet Nam, while Korea and Philippines have industry-led templates. In Pakistan and Malaysia there is no template for corporate bond contracts, however a template for trust deeds exists. Further, the Malaysian Securities Commission clarifies the minimum requirements to be included in the preamble and recitals of the trust deed, such as a brief description of the corporate bonds or sukuk (SC Malaysia, 2020[15]).

Two-thirds of jurisdictions set a time frame for the regulator's approval process. Setting a timeframe for prospectus approval enables corporations to get a clearer outlook on their issuance schedule. In particular, Korea set the maximum time limit for prospectus approval of seven days for publicly offered corporate bonds. Similarly, Australia set an "exposure period" of seven days after the filing of the prospectus. Moreover, Bangladesh also has a comparatively shorter timeframe of 7 working days for private issuance, while for public issuance the regulator can take up to 17 working days to approve the prospectus. The Monetary Authority of Singapore (MAS) indicates a period of 7-21 days for the registration of the prospectus after the submission (MAS, 2020[16]). The regulator in Thailand can take up to 120 days for the approval. The average time for the regulator's approval is around 40 days for the 12 jurisdictions who do set a time limit for the approval.[3]

Figure 3.2. Selected procedures for corporate bond issuances

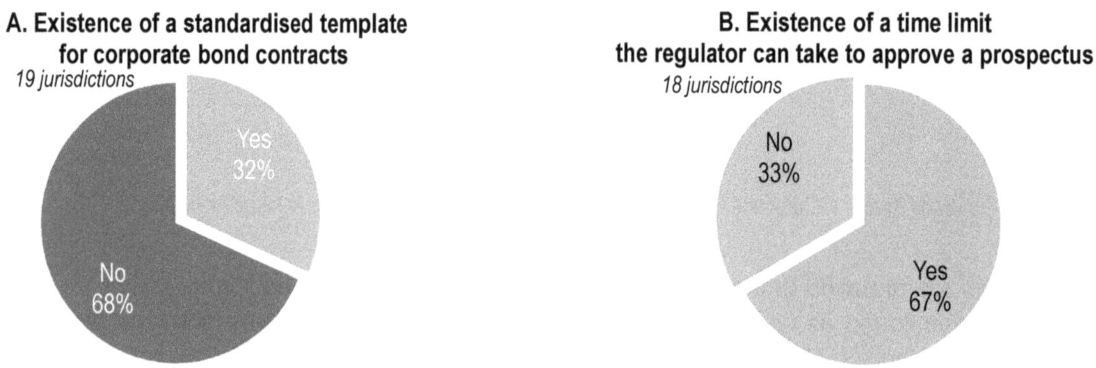

Source: OECD Survey on Access to Corporate Bond Markets for Growth Companies in Asia, see Annex B for details.

Sixteen jurisdictions have a streamlined process for recurrent corporate bond issuers. Usually, this practice aims to facilitate the issuance process for frequent issuers (Figure 3.3). These streamlined processes include allowing issuers to follow simplified procedures, to issue a simplified prospectus or a generic prospectus. Among those jurisdictions with specific provisions, 12 jurisdictions accept a generic prospectus. Frequent issuers can follow simplified procedures in 10 jurisdictions (Indonesia, Japan, Korea, Lao PDR, Mongolia, China, Philippines, Singapore, Chinese Taipei and Thailand), and can issue a simplified prospectus in six jurisdictions (Australia, India, Japan, Lao PDR, Malaysia and Singapore). The Securities and Exchange Commission of the Philippines is considering the implementation of a simplified prospectus procedure. Additionally, Japan, Lao PDR and Singapore accept a generic prospectus and a simplified prospectus, and also offer a simplified procedure for recurrent issuers. In contrast, Bangladesh, Cambodia and Sri Lanka do not have specific provisions for frequent issuers.

Figure 3.3. Specific provisions for frequent corporate bond issuers

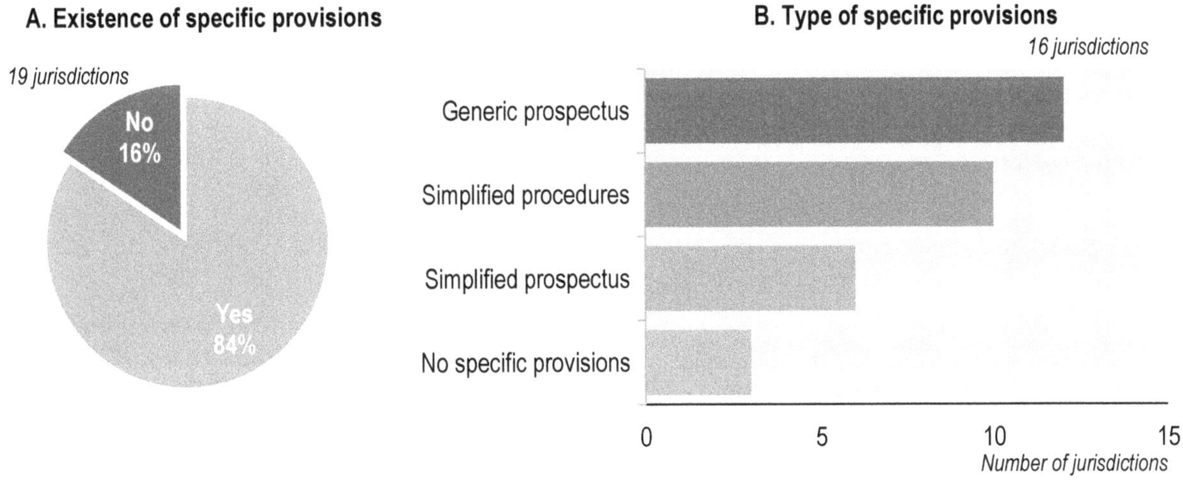

Note: Frequent corporate bond issuers also refer to issuers with bond issuances within a predefined programme. In Panel B, jurisdictions could have provisions regarding several options.
Source: OECD Survey on Access to Corporate Bond Markets for Growth Companies in Asia, see Annex B for details.

Issuances to the public are allowed in the regulatory framework of all jurisdictions and private placements are allowed in almost all jurisdictions. Restrictions apply to smaller companies. For example, SMEs in Indonesia, Philippines and Chinese Taipei are not permitted to publicly issue corporate bonds. Additionally, in Indonesia and Philippines, they are also restricted from raising capital through private placements. Panel A in Figure 3.4 summarises the types of the corporate bond offerings and investors allowed to participate in corporate bond markets in the surveyed jurisdictions. In the Philippines, while the regulatory framework does not use the term “private placements”, it allows a corporate bond to be issued to qualified investors, which in practice functions as private placements (ADB, 2017[4]). In countries like Indonesia, whether companies are allowed to issue via a private placement depends on the type of company. While large companies are allowed to issue to the public and private placements, SMEs are not allowed to publicly nor privately issue corporate bonds. For SMEs, Indonesia has established a crowdfunding platform where these companies can offer debt securities to investors with a simplified procedure.

Bond issuances to domestic qualified investors are allowed in all jurisdictions and **domestic retail investors are permitted to invest in corporate bond markets in 17 jurisdictions**, except in Korea and Viet Nam. Panel B of Figure 3.4 presents the type of investors allowed to participate in corporate bond markets.

While 18 of the jurisdictions allow bond issuances to foreign qualified investors and 15 jurisdictions to non-domestic retail investors, these investors face some restrictions to invest in bonds issued by smaller companies. A few markets are more restrictive when it comes to foreign investors, for example, Lao PDR does not allow corporate bond issuances to any foreign investor. China, Korea and Viet Nam allow non-domestic qualified investors to invest in their local corporate bond market, however, retail foreign investors are prevented from participating in these corporate bond markets. In the Philippines, smaller companies are not allowed to issue corporate bonds to foreign investors.

Figure 3.4. Corporate bonds offering types and investors participating in corporate bond markets

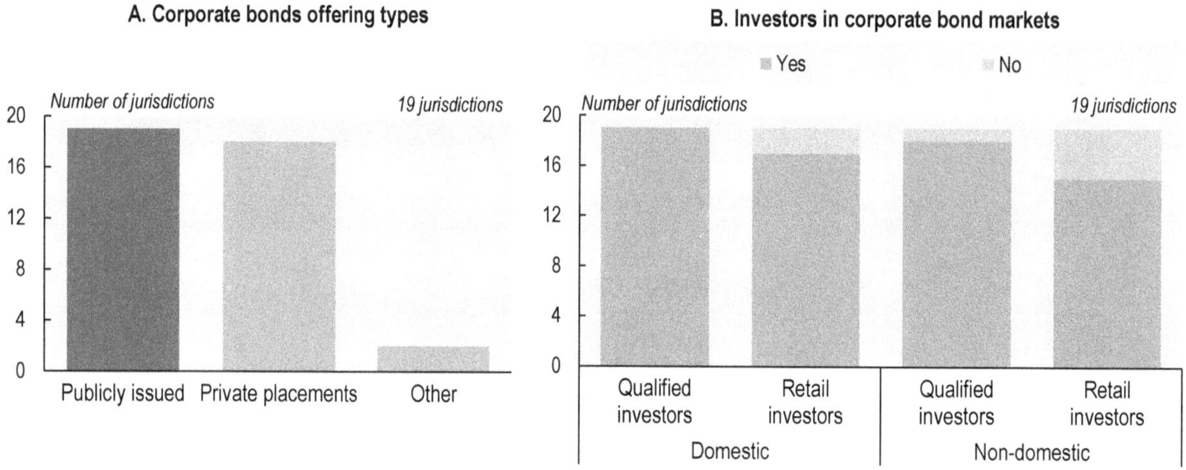

Source: OECD Survey on Access to Corporate Bond Markets for Growth Companies in Asia, see Annex B for details.

3.2. General information on corporate bond markets for growth companies

The definition of growth companies in the regulatory framework differs across surveyed jurisdictions and is usually not used to target policies facilitating growth companies' bond issuance process. **In 17 jurisdictions there is a definition of growth companies or more generally SMEs** (Figure 3.5, Panel A). Cambodia and Sri Lanka have no definition for these companies. The survey investigated different criteria used by jurisdictions to identify a growth company. Among the 17 jurisdictions with criteria defining growth companies, the number of employees is used in 12 jurisdictions and turnover volume by eight jurisdictions (Figure 3.5, Panel B). Total assets and the listing status are used to a lesser extent to define growth companies (see Annex A for details).

Seven jurisdictions have a definition using a criterion different from number of employees, total assets and/or listing status (Figure 3.5, Panel B). For example, Bangladesh, Japan, Pakistan and Chinese Taipei use paid-up capital to define growth companies. In India, companies are defined according to their level of investment in plant and machinery or equipment. Both Korea and Indonesia have criteria on ownership structure in the definition of growth companies. To be defined as a growth company, a company's management has to be independent from other large companies. In addition, China, Hong Kong (China), Japan, Thailand and Viet Nam have different definitions depending on the industry where companies operate.

Figure 3.5. Definition of growth companies

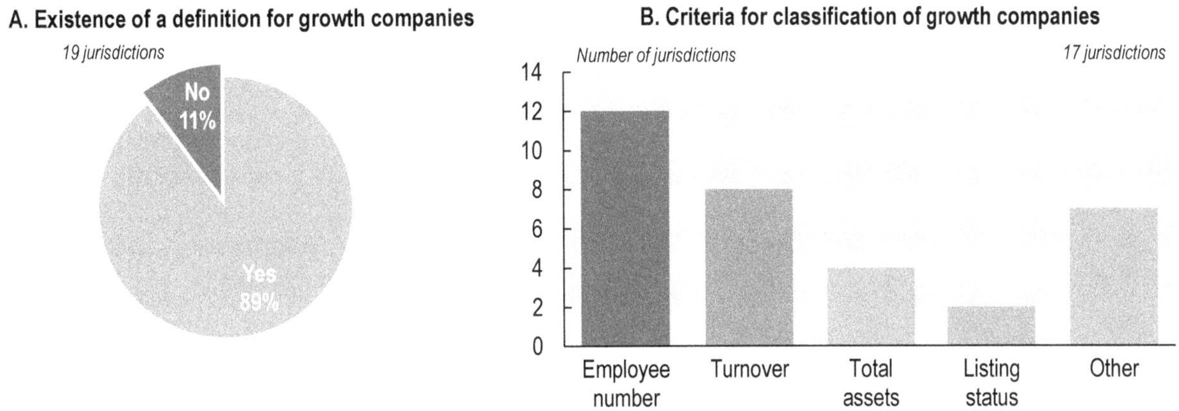

Note: See Annex A for details on the definition of growth companies in selected jurisdictions.
Source: OECD Survey on Access to Corporate Bond Markets for Growth Companies in Asia, see Annex B for details.

In the surveyed jurisdictions it is not common for the application of exemptions in the corporate bond issuance process to promote growth companies' access to market-based financing (Figure 3.6). Only four jurisdictions (Australia, India, Indonesia and Singapore) waive certain requirements or procedures for growth companies. While not perceived as an exemption for smaller companies, Australia allows a simplified prospectus for 'simple corporate bond' issuances over AUD 50 million. This regime allows issuers to use a base prospectus and complement it with an 'offer specific prospectus'. Additionally, corporate bonds must be quoted on an Australian market and the issuer generally must be a listed company that has continuously issued securities or be a wholly-owned subsidiary of a parent entity that has continuously listed securities (Government of Australia, 2001[17]). Another example is India, where there is an exemption for the submission of historical financial statements for newly established corporations. In addition, Indonesia permits growth companies to issue simplified prospectus and require a reduced number of historical financial statements. Singapore waives the submission of prospectus for certain corporate bond issuances, such as a small offer raising no more than 5 million Singaporean dollar within any period of 12 months or private placements offered to no more than 50 investors.

Figure 3.6. Exemptions in place for issuing growth-company bonds

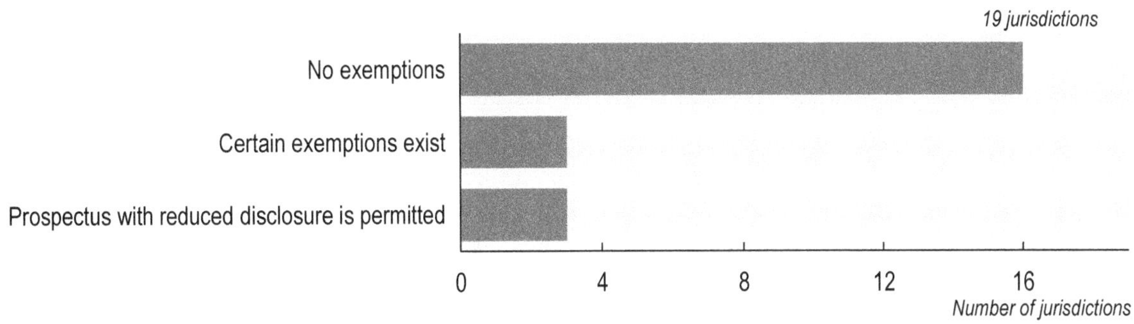

Note: Permission to issue a prospectus with reduced disclosure requirements is shown separately, as it was not pointed out by jurisdictions as an exemption.
Source: OECD Survey on Access to Corporate Bond Markets for Growth Companies in Asia, see Annex B for details.

Thirteen jurisdictions have at least one measure in place to promote access to corporate bond markets (Figure 3.7). As these measures generally aim to increase overall access to corporate bond markets, both large companies and growth companies can benefit from them. In particular, Malaysia introduced the Lodge and Launch framework in 2015 for offerings of unlisted capital markets products, including corporate bonds targeting qualified investors. The system aims to increase efficiency in the issuance process through an online system to submit the relevant information and documents. Additionally, there is an SME-targeted initiative in Korea, led by the Korea SMEs and Startups Agency (KOSME). KOSME supports SMEs that are unable to issue corporate bonds by packaging a large number of bonds issued by SMEs in the form of primary collateralised bond obligation (CBO). Additionally, Japan, Mongolia and Philippines have private initiatives to promote access to corporate bond markets.

Figure 3.7. Specific measures to support access to corporate bond markets

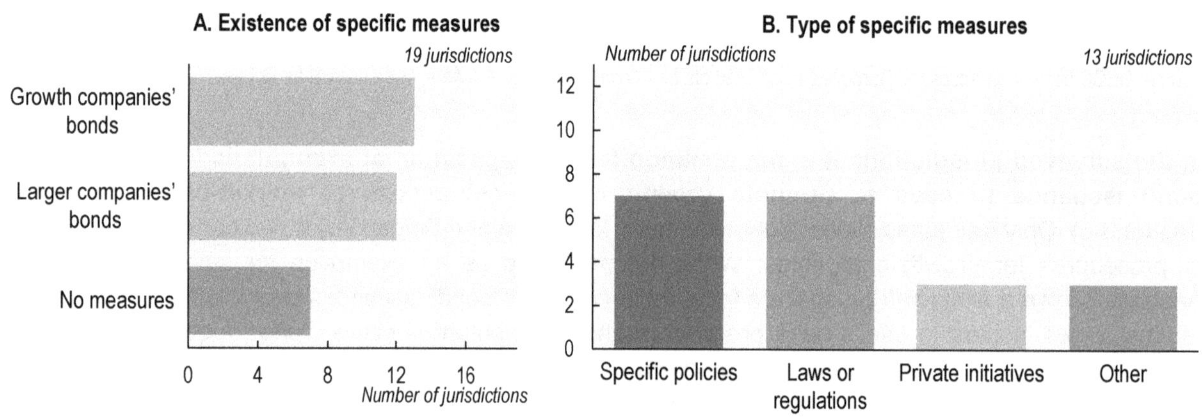

Note: In Panel A, a jurisdiction can have in place measures for growth companies and for large companies at the same time, therefore both categories are not mutually exclusive.
Source: OECD Survey on Access to Corporate Bond Markets for Growth Companies in Asia, see Annex B for details.

3.3. Barriers to access corporate bond markets

Bank lending is the prominent source of financing for corporation in Asia as shown in Chapter 2. Despite the rapid development of corporate bond markets for growth companies, several barriers still impede the further development of corporate bond markets in Asia.

Potential barriers to the development of corporate bond markets include: weak regulatory frameworks, lack of market infrastructure and the presence of intermediaries, a small and unsustainable investor base, high costs and complexity of issuance of bonds compared to bank credit, legal and investor protection issues, corporate governance issues, undeveloped government bond markets, a small number of mature firms and weak disclosure standards (IOSCO, 2015[18]). A number of studies concluded that these barriers seem to be driven by economic size and the level of economic development (World Economic Forum, 2012[19]). For instance, economic size allows for a liquid government bond market, which in turn provides a benchmark yield curve to price corporate bonds. In addition, the larger the economy, the more likely that companies and their financing needs will grow. Larger financing needs are prompting larger bond issuances, which tend to reduce the relative cost of bond financing due to economies of scale. The level of economic development affects the ability of corporations to offer corporate bonds on a continuous basis. Also, weak business and legal environments could negatively affect investor protection and market confidence hindering the growth of corporate bond markets. In addition, the limited size of domestic pension funds, mutual funds and insurance corporations in developing economies may not provide a sufficient investor base limiting the development of corporate bond markets.

Seventeen jurisdictions identified the limited liquidity of corporate bonds as a main barrier (Figure 3.8). The limited liquidity of corporate bonds contributes to undermine the attractiveness of corporate bond investments for certain investors (Bessembinder et al., 2018[20]). Recent evidence suggests that corporate bond markets are less liquid than some other traded markets and the number of individual corporate debt securities that trade regularly is small at a global scale (IOSCO, 2022[21]). Nevertheless, it is challenging to assess whether corporate bond market liquidity is primarily undermined by the lack of liquidity supply by dealers, increased liquidity demand by investors, or a combination of both factors.

Assessment of the creditworthiness of companies has been identified by 14 jurisdictions as a main barrier to the development of corporate bond markets. Challenges in evaluating credit worthiness undermine investors' ability to accurately evaluate risks and, therefore, it affects their willingness to invest in assets. As discussed in Chapter 5, domestic and regional CRAs are operating in all surveyed jurisdictions, and alternative credit systems have been developed in some jurisdictions. Nevertheless, these results suggest that more efforts are needed to better assess issuers' credit risk to investors to effectively support corporate bond issuance in Asia.

Figure 3.8. Main barriers to non-financial companies issuing corporate bonds

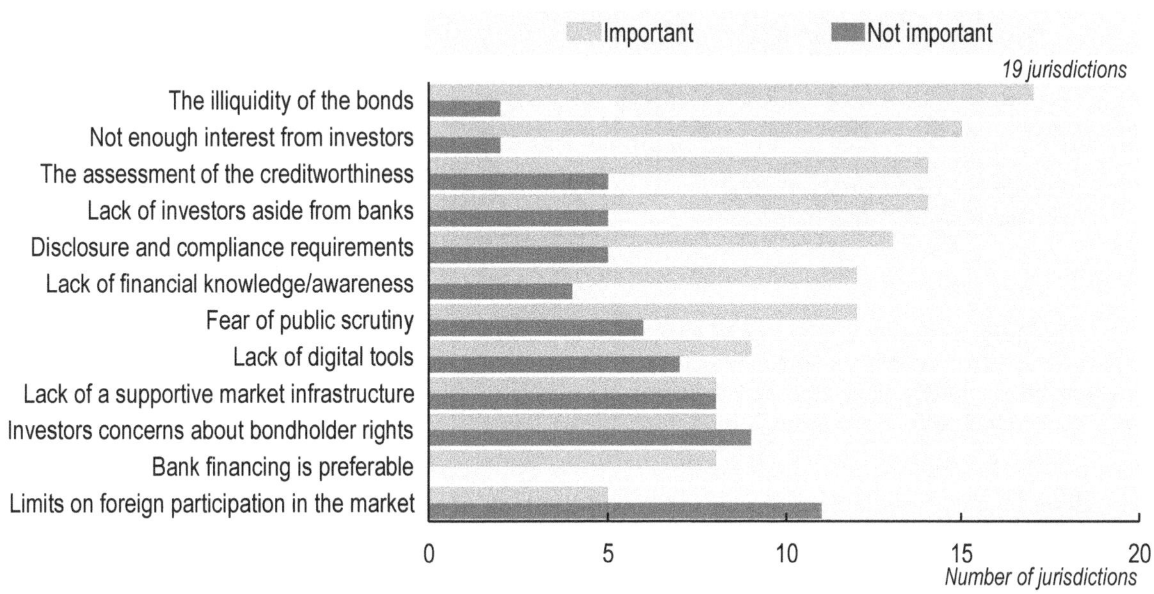

Source: OECD Survey on Access to Corporate Bond Markets for Growth Companies in Asia, see Annex B for details.

The lack of investors, aside from banks, was identified as the fourth most important barrier and echoes the lack of interest from investors to invest in corporate bonds. The possible lack of investors (aside from banks) could be mitigated by the contribution of institutional investors in many Asian jurisdictions. However, despite the significant size of Asian institutional investors they do not play a significant role in regional corporate bond markets. At the end of 2022, assets under management of the top 300 pension funds totalled USD 20.6 trillion globally and Asia-Pacific accounted for 26.4% of these assets (Thinking Ahead Institute and Pensions & Investments, 2023[22]). As a comparison, the United Stated and Europe represented 45.6% and 24.1% of world's 300 largest pension funds' assets, respectively. Similarly, the total assets of insurance companies in Asia accounted for 27% of world's total in 2021, compared to 34% in the United States and 39% in Europe and Africa (International Association of Insurance Supervisors, 2022[23]).

Twelve jurisdictions identified the lack of financial knowledge and awareness of investors in the region as important barriers. Lack of awareness likely contributes to undermine investors' ability to assess the benefits and risks of corporate bond investments, therefore potentially limiting the expansion of corporate bond markets in certain jurisdictions. Indeed, financial literacy deficiencies could limit investors' interest in buying relatively risky and complex corporate bonds. As shown in Figure 3.9, in several jurisdictions, the share of the adult population assessed as financially literate was below the world average score of 33.

Figure 3.9. Financial literacy indicator for selected jurisdictions

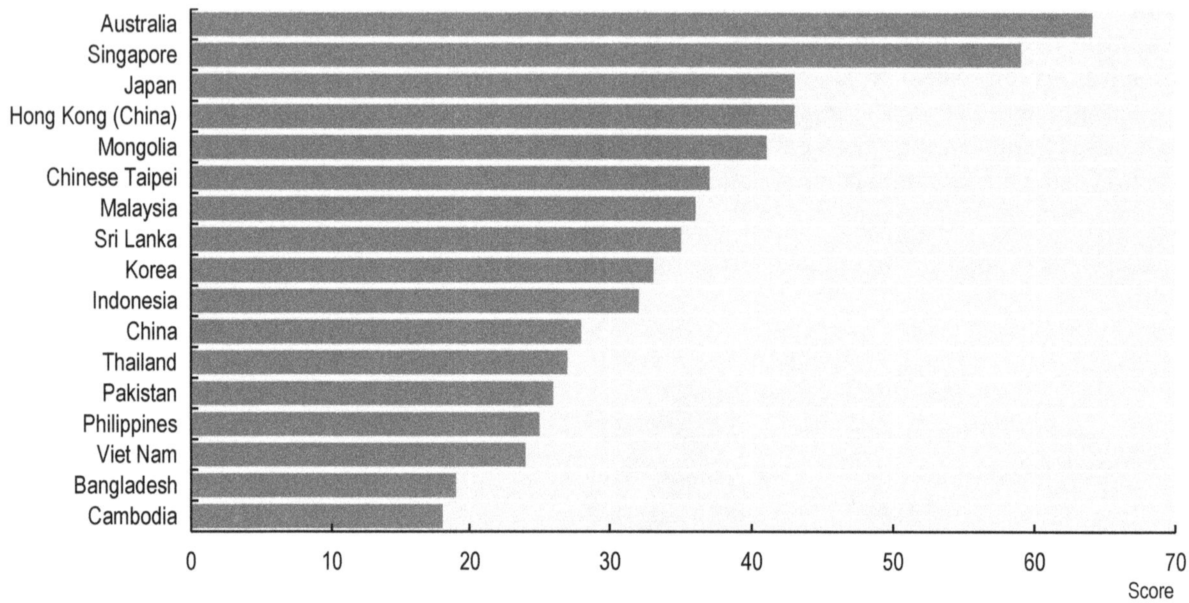

Note: This Figure shows the share of adults who are financially literate by country in 2014. Data are not available for India and Lao PDR. In the S&P Global FinLit Survey, the literacy questions measure the four fundamental concepts for financial decision making that include basic numeracy, interest compounding, inflation and risk diversification.
Source: (Klapper, Lusardi and Van Oudheusden, 2014[24]).

Other barriers such as the **lack of digital tools and the lack of supportive market infrastructure have been identified as impediments in nine and eight jurisdictions**, respectively. Asia is already a leader in digital innovation, and efforts towards economic readiness for digitalisation have been substantive in several jurisdictions, particularly in China and Japan (Figure 3.10). Nevertheless, further efforts to develop the array of digitalisation tools could enhance the involvement of a variety of market participants, notably in corporate bond markets. It is worth noting that the lack of supportive market infrastructure in terms of relevant technological or human resources (e.g. skilled accountants and lawyers at underwriting companies such as investment banks) could hinder the feasibility of issuance, the expansion of the market and subsequently market liquidity. Despite the prominence of bank loan financing in Asia, **only eight of the jurisdictions surveyed have identified a preference for bank financing as a barrier to the development of corporate bond markets.**

Corporate governance issues, including challenges from fear of public scrutiny, disclosure and compliance requirements and, to a lesser extent, investors' concerns about bondholder rights were also identified as barriers.

Figure 3.10. Economic readiness index for digitalisation in selected jurisdictions, 2022

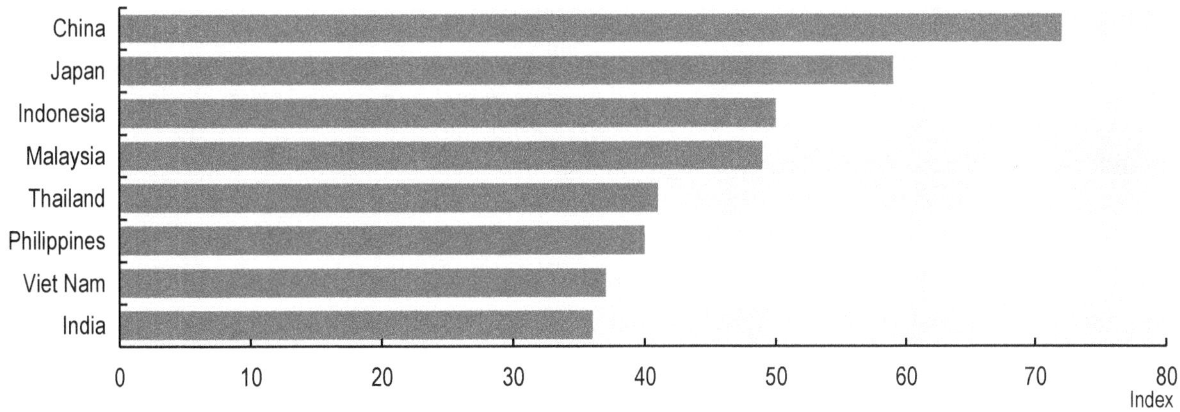

Note: This Figure shows economic readiness index for digitalisation in selected jurisdictions. This index measures overall progress in macroeconomic readiness to foster digitalisation, scoring each country out of 100. Data are as of 2022.
Source: (Asia House, 2022[25]).

Finally, **limits on foreign participations in the market have been identified as a barrier by five jurisdictions**. As documented in this chapter, a number of jurisdictions allow the issuance of corporate bonds to foreign qualified investors, and also to non-domestic retail investors. Therefore, limits on foreign participation tend to be less of an obstacle to corporate bond issuance in a number of jurisdictions. Nevertheless, capital control measures implemented in certain jurisdictions could discourage foreign investors' participation and limit the expansion of corporate bond markets in the region (World Bank, 2023[26]).

3.4. Tax treatment of corporate bonds

The tax treatment of corporate bonds, both from the perspective of issuers and investors, is an important component that could play a role in the development of corporate bond markets. While the specifics vary across jurisdictions, generally there are three taxing points for a corporate bond investor: when interest is earned on the bond; when there are capital gains or losses earned in the sale of the bond; and through an original issue discount (i.e. when the bond is issued for less than its face value). From the issuer perspective, in general the interest paid to bondholders can be deducted as expense against corporate income. Overall, the tax treatment for investors of corporate bonds is similar in structure in Asia and differs in terms of the rates and conditions applied.

The tax paid on the interest received by investors from holding corporate bonds is common across 17 jurisdictions. This tax is not applied in Lao PDR and only in certain circumstances in Hong Kong (China) and Mongolia (Table 3.1). When it comes to the different applications in these jurisdictions, for example, in India, the tax rate that applies to interest payments from holding corporate bonds depends on the marginal tax rate of the taxpayer (Government of India, 1961[27]). In Chinese Taipei, for companies investing in corporate bonds, the interest income is taxed at the company's corporate income tax. In Korea, individuals and foreign investors pay the same tax rate on interest payments from holding corporate bonds. In Pakistan, the tax on interest payments received by investors varies depending on if the instrument is sukuk (10-25%) or debt including corporate bonds (15%), with the tax rate depending on the size of the return and whether the investor is an individual or a company (Goverment of Pakistan, 2001[28]). In Mongolia, a 5% tax on interest payments received by bondholders only applies to interest received in relation to publicly offered bonds. In Hong Kong (China), the interest income derived from certain debt instruments is exempt from profits tax for corporations (Hong Kong (China), 1947[29]).

Capital gains tax is applied to a lesser extent in only 14 jurisdictions. However, the rate applied in Korea and Singapore is 0% (Table 3.1). While the specifics vary across jurisdictions, when an investor sells the corporate bond before its maturity date, and the amount an investor receives is above the original purchase price of the bond, the difference can be considered to be a capital gain and this gain is taxed in some jurisdictions. However, the income derived may not necessarily be treated as capital gains but rather income.[4] Hong Kong (China), Lao PDR, Malaysia and Chinese Taipei do not tax the gains derived from such transactions. For example, Chinese Taipei ceased to impose an income tax on gains derived from securities transactions since 1990. In Pakistan, for listed instruments, the capital gains tax rate is 5%-15% depending upon the holding period. For unlisted instruments the rate is 3.5% to 15% depending upon the gain (Part V 37, (Goverment of Pakistan, 2001[28]).

Ten jurisdictions (Australia, Japan, Korea, Mongolia, Philippines, Singapore, Sri Lanka, Chinese Taipei, Thailand and Viet Nam jurisdictions) **apply a withholding tax to foreign resident investors in relation to any interest earned or on disposal of the bond**. A common rationale for governments to apply withholding taxes on foreign resident investors is that if foreign investors are not taxed by the source country, then the investor would benefit from the infrastructure of the source country without contributing to it by paying other taxes. Further, this type of tax is relatively straightforward for the tax authority to administer because they already interact with the issuer companies, while they may not interact with the non-resident investors (Petkova, 2020[30]). Generally, the liability to withhold tax generally arises when the interest or gain made from holding the bond has been paid to the foreign resident. This tax must be withheld by the bond issuer and remitted by the bond issuer to the source jurisdiction taxation authority. For example, in the Philippines, a final withholding tax is withheld at every coupon payment date and remitted to the Bureau of Internal Revenue by the issuer (Philippines Bureau of Internal Revenue, 2023[31]).

However, the withholding tax for foreign investors may be waived whenever there a double taxation agreement, which is common in many countries (Table 3.1). Some jurisdictions have treaties to ensure that there is not double taxation on earnings by foreign investors. That is, when a jurisdiction applies a withholding tax on a foreign investor and the resident jurisdiction also taxes the same earnings, the double taxation agreement generally means that the source jurisdiction does not apply withholding tax on the income. For example, in Mongolia, the withholding tax of 20% for foreign investors applies only when there is no double taxation agreement in place with a foreign jurisdiction. Similarly, in Korea, the withholding tax rate of 15.4% for foreign investors may vary depending on their country's tax treaty with Korea. Another example is in Japan, where the withholding tax rate depend on the existence of a tax treaty in effect between Japan and the country of residence of non-resident individual or the country where the foreign corporation is located.

Several jurisdictions have tax exemptions in place to help attracting investors and investment. In Thailand, the 15% withholding tax for individual foreign investors does not apply for zero coupon bonds. Additionally, in Bangladesh, the original issue discount[5] that investors make on their investment in zero coupon bonds is tax exempt.[6] There are specific exemptions from interest withholding tax for corporate bonds in Australia and Singapore. For instance, section 128F of the (Australian Parliament, 1936[32]) in Australia provides an exemption from interest withholding tax for offers of public placements of corporate bonds under AUD 100 million, if certain requirements are met. To qualify for the exemption, the borrower must satisfy one of five public offer tests, for example, the offer must be genuinely made to at least 10 unrelated investors or offered publicly in an electronic form. Similarly, in Singapore, for debt instruments under the Qualifying Debt Securities (QDS) scheme, the income derived by an entity operating in Singapore is subject to tax at a concessionary tax rate of 10%, and similarly to the Australian exemption, interest derived by non-residents is (Government of Singapore, 1947[33]; 2001[34]). Similarly, Hong Kong (China) also has Qualifying Debt Instrument concession and exemption scheme (Inland Revenue Department, Hong Kong (China), 2021[35]). In summary, typically, to access these exemption, public offers of the bonds must be made, and in some cases accepted by a certain number of investors, and the parties buying the bonds cannot be related to the issuing company to access these tax concession or exemptions.

Table 3.1. Tax treatment for holders of corporate bonds

Jurisdiction	Tax on interest payments	Capital gains taxation (CGT) rate[1]	Withholding tax (WHT) for foreign investors[2]
Australia	Individual: marginal tax rate Large company: 30% SME: 25%	Individual: marginal tax rate Large company: 30% SME: 25%	0%-10% (public offer exception)
Bangladesh	5% on coupons / 2% on perpetual bonds (mainly issued by financial institutions in the form of Additional Tier-1 capital)	0-10% (zero coupon bond exemption)	No WHT
Cambodia	20% standard rate, or 10% with tax incentive for listed issuers	20% (currently listed bonds are exempt)	14% standard rate, or 7% on interest from securities from listed issuers
China	Individual: 20% Company: 25% (exception for perpetual bonds)	Individual: 20% Company: 25%	10%, or 5% for bonds regularly traded on recognised exchanges
Hong Kong (China)	0% / 16.5% (subject to two-tier rate) (Qualifying Debt Instruments concession/exemption or exempt per Unified Fund Regime if under the 5% cap)	No CGT	No WHT
India	Taxpayers' marginal tax rate	Long-term capital gains tax: 20% Short-term capital gains tax: marginal tax rate	5%
Indonesia	10%	-	10%
Japan	20.315%	20.315%	15.315%
Korea	Individual: 15.4% (income tax 14%; local tax 1.4%)	0%	Individual: 15.4% (income tax 14%; local tax 1.4%)
Lao PDR	No tax on interest payments	No CGT	Not applicable
Malaysia	-	No CGT	-
Mongolia	5% (publicly offered bonds only)	10%	20%
Pakistan	12.5%-25%	3.5%-15%	Not applicable
Philippines	20%	7%	Individuals: 25% Companies: 30%
Singapore	10-17% (Qualifying Debt Securities concession)	0%	0-15% (Qualifying Debt Securities exception)
Sri Lanka	5%	10%	5%
Chinese Taipei	Individual: 10% Company: corporate tax rate	No CGT	15%
Thailand	Individual: 15% Company: 1% withholding tax and included in corporate income tax	Individual: 0-15% Company: 0% or corporate tax rate (zero coupon bond exemption)	Individuals: 0-15% Companies: 0-15% (zero coupon bond exemption)
Viet Nam	Corporate tax rate	20%	Corporate tax at a deemed rate of 0.1% of the gross sales proceeds

Note: Surveyed jurisdictions were asked if there was a difference between the taxation rate for large and growth companies, however for most jurisdictions the rate was the same. Withholding tax for foreign investors assumes that a double taxation agreement does not apply.
1. indicates that while CGT may apply in a jurisdiction more broadly, it does not necessarily apply to gains relating to corporate bonds.
2. indicates that double tax agreements may be in place in many jurisdictions, meaning that WHT is not applied.
"–" indicates where a response to the OECD survey was not provided by the jurisdiction and further research was not conclusive.
Source: OECD Survey on Access to Corporate Bond Markets for Growth Companies in Asia, see Annex B for details. In some cases additional research sources were used: Cambodia (ADB, 2018[36]; KPMG, 2023[37]); China (PwC, 2023[38]; EY, 2019[39]); Malaysia (PwC, 2023[38]); India (Government of India, 1961[27]); Indonesia (PwC, 2023[38]; ADB, 2021[5]); Sri Lanka (PwC, 2023[38]).

Consistent with the general tax-deductibility of interest payments in tax frameworks, **16 jurisdictions allow for the tax deductibility of interest paid to bondholders by the issuer**. In addition, only two jurisdictions (Australia and Thailand) provide corporate bond issuers with certain tax measures in relation to the costs they incur in raising debt (Figure 3.11). In Australia, borrowing costs (other than interest) that are incurred to produce assessable income are also generally deductible, such as the costs involved to issue corporate bonds (Sobeck, 2022[40]; Thomson Reuters, 2021[41]). Similarly, in Thailand, expenses incurred in the bond issuance process are allowed as a deduction (KPMG, 2018[42]). In Hong Kong (China), interest paid to bondholders by the issuer is tax deductible subject to certain conditions. In Malaysia, a special regime for sukuk was instituted to align the tax treatment of Islamic finance bonds to that of regular bonds. As such, there are various tax incentives available for sukuk, for example stamp duty exemptions for the issuance process and a tax deduction for the expenditure incurred by the issuer of a Sustainable and Responsible Investment (SRI) sukuk (SEC, 2023[43]).

Some jurisdictions have also implemented tax reductions for corporations who list their corporate bonds, to incentivise this type of activity. For example, in Lao PDR, companies that list their securities on the Lao Securities Exchange (LSX) can benefit from a 5% profit tax reduction for four years (ADB, 2017[44]).

In general, the application of taxes and the rate of these taxes varies across jurisdictions responding to the OECD Survey (Table 3.1). However, in Asia, there is not a difference in the tax treatment of smaller and larger companies in relation to holders of corporate bonds. An exception is Australia, where the capital gains tax rate paid by SMEs is a lower rate of 25%, while larger companies pay 30% (this simply reflects the different corporate tax rates that apply in this jurisdiction).

Aside from tax related exemptions and deductibility, jurisdictions also provide other measures to support the corporate bond markets. For instance, to promote the green bond market in Hong Kong (China), the Government Green Bond Programme was introduced in 2018 to help set a benchmark for green bond products in the market and provide good examples for potential green issuers. In addition, a three-year Green and Sustainable Finance Grant Scheme was announced in the 2021-22 budget to provide a subsidy for eligible bond issuers to cover their expenses for bond issuance and external review services. In the year following the launch of the scheme, almost 100 green and sustainable debt instruments were issued in Hong Kong (China) and were granted subsidies for the bond issuance costs or external review, with the total underlying issuance being around USD 30 billion (Hong Kong (China), 2021[45]; 2022[46]). Similarly, Indonesia reduced the registration fee for green bonds to be 75% lower than the normal rate for the public offering of bonds (ADB, 2021[5]).

Figure 3.11. Tax treatment of corporate bond issuers

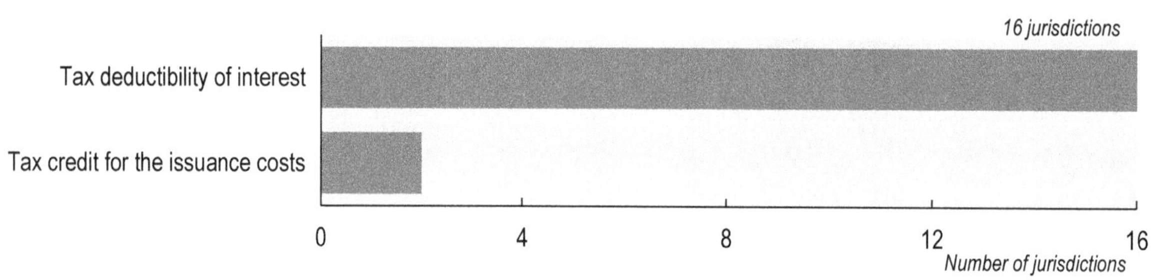

Source: OECD Survey on Access to Corporate Bond Markets for Growth Companies in Asia, see Annex B for details.

References

ADB (2021), *The Bond Market in Indonesia*, https://asianbondsonline.adb.org/documents/abmf_ino_bond_market_guide_2021.pdf. [5]

ADB (2021), *The Bond Market in Thailand: An ASEAN+3 Bond Market Guide Update*, https://doi.org/10.22617/TCS210470-2. [3]

ADB (2018), *ASEAN+3 Bond Market Guide 2018: Republic of Korea*, https://doi.org/10.22617/TCS189302-2. [6]

ADB (2018), *Cambodia Bond Market Guide*, https://doi.org/10.22617/TCS189196-2. [36]

ADB (2017), *ASEAN+3 Bond Market Guide 2017: Indonesia*, https://doi.org/10.22617/TCS178908-2. [10]

ADB (2017), *ASEAN+3 Bond Market Guide 2017: Philippines*, https://asianbondsonline.adb.org/documents/abmf_phi_bond_market_guide_2017.pdf. [4]

ADB (2017), *Bond Market Guide Lao PDR*, https://asianbondsonline.adb.org/documents/abmg/abmf_lao_bmg2017-chp6.pdf. [44]

Asia House (2022), *Annual Outlook 2022*, https://asiahouse.org/wp-content/uploads/2022/01/Asia-House-Annual-Outlook-2022.pdf. [25]

Australian Parliament (2021), *The Development of the Australian Corporate Bond Market: A Way Forward*, https://parlinfo.aph.gov.au/parlInfo/download/committees/reportrep/024469/toc_pdf/TheDevelopmentoftheAustralianCorporateBondMarketAWayForward.pdf;fileType=application%2Fpdf. [47]

Australian Parliament (1936), *Income Tax Assessment Act 1936*, https://www.legislation.gov.au/Series/C1936A00027. [32]

Bessembinder, H. et al. (2018), *Capital Commitment and Illiquidity in Corporate Bonds*, The Journal of Finance, 73(4), 1615–1661, http://www.jstor.org/stable/26654661. [20]

Cambodia Securities Exchange (2017), *Debt Securities Listing Rules of the Cambodia Securities Exchange*, http://csx.com.kh/file/eng/rules_lsr/2020/Amended%20Debt%20Securities%20Listing%20Rules.pdf. [11]

Dhaka Stock Exchange (2015), *Dhaka Stock Exchange (Listing) Regulations, 2015*, https://www.dsebd.org/assets/pdf/listing_reg_2015.pdf. [12]

EY (2019), *China releases the corporate income tax treatment on perpetual bonds*, https://www.ey.com/en_gl/tax-alerts/china-releases-the-corporate-income-tax-treatment-on-perpetual-bonds. [39]

Goverment of Pakistan (2001), *Income Tax Ordinance*, https://www.fbr.gov.pk/Categ/Income-Tax-Ordinance/326. [28]

Government of Australia (2001), *Corporations Act 2001 (No. 50)*, https://www.legislation.gov.au/Details/C2023C00194. [17]

Government of India (1961), *Income Tax Act*, https://incometaxindia.gov.in/pages/acts/income-tax-act.aspx. [27]

Government of Singapore (2001), *Income Tax (Qualifying Debt Securities) Regulations*, https://sso.agc.gov.sg/SL/ITA1947-RG35?DocDate=20181227. [34]

Government of Singapore (1947), *Income Tax Act 1947*, https://sso.agc.gov.sg/Act/ITA1947. [33]

Hong Kong (China) (2022), *Report of the Steering Committee on Bond Market Development in Hong Kong*, https://www.fstb.gov.hk/fsb/en/publication/report/docs/Report%20of%20the%20Steering%20Committee%20on%20Bond%20Market%20Development%20in%20Hong%20Kong_EN_2022_08.pdf. [46]

Hong Kong (China) (2021), *The 2021-22 Budget*, https://www.budget.gov.hk/2021/eng/index.html. [45]

Hong Kong (China) (1947), *Inland Revenue Ordinance (Cap 112)*, https://www.elegislation.gov.hk/hk/cap112. [29]

Inland Revenue Department, Hong Kong (China) (2021), *FAQ: Qualifying Debt Instruments*, https://www.ird.gov.hk/eng/faq/qdi.htm. [35]

International Association of Insurance Supervisors (2022), *Global Insurance Market Report (GIMAR)*, https://www.iaisweb.org/uploads/2022/12/GIMAR-2022.pdf. [23]

IOSCO (2022), *Corporate Bond Markets – Drivers of Liquidity During COVID-19 Induced Market Stresses*, https://www.iosco.org/library/pubdocs/pdf/IOSCOPD700.pdf. [21]

IOSCO (2015), *Corporate Bond Markets: An Emerging Markets Perspective*, Staff Working Paper of the IOSCO Research Department, https://www.iosco.org/library/pubdocs/pdf/IOSCOPD510.pdf. [18]

Klapper, L., A. Lusardi and P. Van Oudheusden (2014), *Financial Literacy Around the World: Insights from the S&P Ratings services global financial literacy survey*, Washington, D.C.: World Bank Group, https://gflec.org/wp-content/uploads/2015/11/3313-Finlit_Report_FINAL-5.11.16.pdf. [24]

KPMG (2023), *Investing in Cambodia*, https://assets.kpmg.com/content/dam/kpmg/kh/pdf/publication/2023/kpmg-investing-in-cambodia-2023-and-beyond.pdf. [37]

KPMG (2018), *Thailand Tax Profile*, https://assets.kpmg.com/content/dam/kpmg/xx/pdf/2018/09/thailand-2018.pdf. [42]

Lao Securities Commission (2014), *Regulation on Issuance of Corporate Bonds*, https://lsc.gov.la/Doc_legal/Regulation%20on%20Issuance%20of%20Corporate%20Bonds.pdf. [2]

Lao Securities Exchange (2023), *Corporate Bond and Government Bond Listing Regulation*, http://www.lsx.com.la/rules/regulations/listPosts.do?lang=en. [13]

Lao Securities Exchange (2011), *Listing on LSX*, http://www.lsx.com.la/en/product/listing.jsp. [9]

MAS (2020), *CIS Practice Note 1/2005, Administrative Procedures for Retail Schemes*, https://www.mas.gov.sg/-/media/MAS/resource/legislation_guidelines/securities_futures/sub_legislation/CIS-Practice-Note-13-March-2020.pdf. [16]

Mongolian Stock Exchange (2018), *Mongolian Stock Exchange Listing Rules*, https://mse.mn/uploads/laws/MSE%20Listing%20Rules%20ENG.pdf. [14]

Petkova, K. (2020), "Withholding tax rates on dividends: symmetries versus asymmetries or single- versus multi-rated double tax treaties", https://link.springer.com/article/10.1007/s10797-020-09637-y. [30]

Philippines Bureau of Internal Revenue (2023), *Withholding Tax*, https://www.bir.gov.ph/index.php/tax-information/withholding-tax.html (accessed on September 2023). [31]

PwC (2023), *Worldwide Tax Summaries*, https://taxsummaries.pwc.com. [38]

SC Malaysia (2022), *Guidelines on Issuance of Corporate Bonds and Sukuk to Retail Investors*, https://www.sc.com.my/api/documentms/download.ashx?id=25454f9f-77b6-4b67-85e6-f1b34d48fb94. [7]

SC Malaysia (2021), *Guidelines on Issuance of Corporate Bonds and Sukuk to Retail Investors*, https://www.sc.com.my/api/documentms/download.ashx?id=5b225f06-2f1f-4d62-afef-a5702bc8bcca. [1]

SC Malaysia (2020), *Guidelines on Trust Deeds*, https://www.sc.com.my/regulation/guidelines/bonds-and-sukuk. [15]

SEBI (2019), *Issue and Listing of Municipal Debt Securities Regulations*, https://www.sebi.gov.in/legal/regulations/sep-2019/securities-and-exchange-board-of-india-issue-and-listing-of-municipal-debt-securities-regulations-2015-last-amended-on-september-27-2019-_34611.html. [8]

SEC (2023), *Islamic Capital Market: Incentives*, Securities Commission Malaysia, https://www.sc.com.my/development/icm/incentives (accessed on September 2023). [43]

Sobeck, K. (2022), *Corporate income taxation in Australia: Theory, current practice and future policy direction*, The Tax and Transfer Policy Institute, https://taxpolicy.crawford.anu.edu.au/sites/default/files/uploads/taxstudies_crawford_anu_edu_au/2022-03/ttpi_corporate_income_tax_report.pdf. [40]

Thinking Ahead Institute and Pensions & Investments (2023), *Global top 300 pension funds study*, http://file:///C:/Users/Roulet_C/Downloads/PI-300-2023-3.pdf. [22]

Thomson Reuters (2021), *Tax on Corporate Lending and Bond Issues in Australia: Overview*, https://uk.practicallaw.thomsonreuters.com/1-520-6118?transitionType=Default&contextData=(sc.Default)&firstPage=true. [41]

World Bank (2023), *Expanding Opportunities: Toward Inclusive Growth. South Asia Economic Focus*, World Bank, Washington, DC., https://openknowledge.worldbank.org/handle/10986/39613. [26]

World Economic Forum (2012), *Redefining the Emerging Market Opportunity, Chapter 4: The Opportunity in Corporate Bonds*, Boston Consulting Group. [19]

Notes

[1] 19 jurisdictions responded to the survey namely Australia, Bangladesh, Cambodia, Hong Kong (China), India, Indonesia, Japan, Korea, Lao PDR, Malaysia, Mongolia, Pakistan, China, Philippines, Singapore, Sri Lanka, Chinese Taipei, Thailand and Viet Nam. The OECD survey was conducted in the first half of 2023.

[2] 17 jurisdictions responded to the relevant question namely, Australia, Bangladesh, Cambodia, India, Indonesia, Korea, Lao PDR, Malaysia, Mongolia, Pakistan, China, Philippines, Singapore, Sri Lanka, Chinese Taipei, Thailand and Viet Nam.

[3] 12 jurisdictions provided information on the number of days allowed for a prospectus approval: Australia, Bangladesh, Cambodia, China, Indonesia, Korea, Lao PDR, Mongolia, Philippines, Singapore, Chinese Taipei and Thailand.

[4] For example, in Australia, a parliamentary inquiry noted: "Tax implications and consequences from proceeds (gains or losses) made from the disposal of corporate bonds may vary depending on individual circumstances and the type of investor... The profit from the redemption of corporate bonds is generally treated as 'other income' and not treated as concessionally taxed capital gains. Conversely, where there [is] a loss made on redemption, a 'revenue' deduction can be claimed and no capital loss recognised. (Australian Parliament, 2021[47])

[5] The difference between the par value and initial price of the bond.

[6] Except if the investor is a bank, non-bank financial institution or insurance company.

4 Marketplaces for corporate bonds in Asia

This chapter focusses on key aspects of marketplaces for corporate bonds, benefiting from the insights of the OECD Survey conducted among 19 regulators from 18 Asian jurisdictions and Australia. It covers issues such as listing fees, derivative markets, market makers, government bond markets and research on growth companies.

Marketplaces for corporate bond issuances and trading, along with securities designed to hedge associated risks, are essential in supporting company financing and enhancing the attractiveness of bond markets for investors. In Asia, many jurisdictions made great efforts to develop their fixed income markets to provide corporations with an important source of funding. The OECD Survey explores these aspects of the marketplaces for corporate bonds in Asia.

4.1. Marketplaces to list and trade corporate bonds

Sixteen[1] jurisdictions have a dedicated segment for corporate bonds on their stock exchange, except for Thailand and Philippines. And **thirteen jurisdictions reported having OTC markets**, only Bangladesh, Lao PDR, China and Sri Lanka do not have an OTC market (Figure 4.1, Panel A).

Some jurisdictions have also implemented special markets. For example, in the Philippines the Dealing Exchange, an electronic trading platform for fixed-income instruments, plays a key role as a dedicated fixed income exchange and over-the-counter market operator. India has an alternative platform for corporate bonds which is called "Request for Quote". On the platform, participants request a quote from multiple counterparts, and then negotiate and confirm the trade. Malaysia has both an exchange and an OTC market for corporate bonds. In addition to these marketplaces, the Malaysian Securities Commission has also introduced a regulatory framework for a peer-to-peer financing (P2P). On the electronic P2P platform, companies can access market-based financing to fund their projects or businesses. Indonesia offers a dedicated fundraising method for SMEs. In 2018, the Indonesian authority established securities crowdfunding. The scope of the crowdfunding was initially restricted to equity, but it expanded to include debt securities and sukuk in 2020. Companies that can use securities crowdfunding are limited to smaller companies, based on criteria related to ownership and asset size.[2] In contrast to standard bond issuance arrangements such as public offerings or private placements, offerors of debt securities are not required to obtain a credit rating. Moreover, the appointment of a trustee, which is also a requirement for a standard procedure, is not necessary for securities crowdfunding (OJK, 2020[1]; 2020[2]).

Figure 4.1. Marketplaces to list and trade corporate bonds

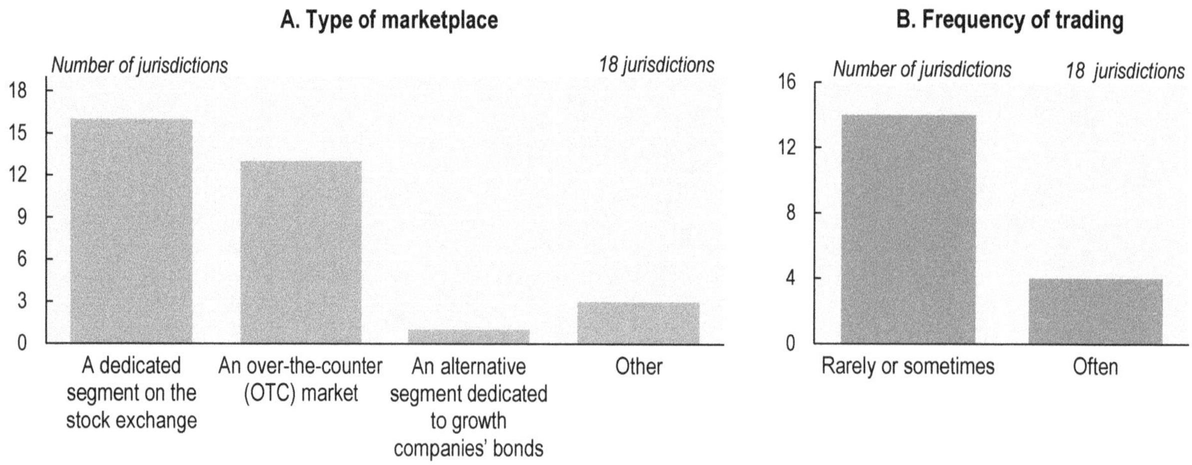

Source: OECD Survey on Access to Corporate Bond Markets for Growth Companies in Asia, see Annex B for details.

Asian corporate bond markets are characterised by low secondary market liquidity, with regulators from only four jurisdictions (Indonesia, Malaysia, Chinese Taipei and Viet Nam) mentioning that large-company bonds are "often" traded in the secondary markets (Figure 4.1, Panel B). Japan, Korea and Singapore acknowledged that the secondary market for large-company bonds is more liquid than the one for growth-company bonds.

Most corporate bonds are primarily traded OTC and do not trade daily. Therefore, the lack of frequent pricing of corporate bonds can make it challenging for investors to access information about these securities and therefore discourage them to invest and trade. Moreover, lack of market prices could make pricing of the holdings in investors' balance sheets very difficult. To facilitate transparency, regulators and self-regulatory organisations (SROs) often require the reporting of detailed trade information, and therefore they try ensuring that this information is disseminated to market participants. Common practice includes the reporting of reference prices or bid and ask prices before a trade is executed. The financial authority in Korea introduced a bond pricing agency that provides mark-to-market information on various bonds, including corporate bonds, to the market. In Indonesia, for example, reference pricing is reported through an electronic platform and disseminated by the Indonesian Bond Pricing Agency (IBPA). Additionally, other transaction details such as the transaction price, yield, and volume of the bonds must be reported and are made public immediately after the transaction (ICMA, 2022[3]; OJK, 2015[4]). In Japan, OTC transaction information is shared via the website of the Japan Securities Dealers Association (JSDA), an SRO, while transactions on the exchange are disseminated through the Japan Exchange Group (JSDA, 2019[5]).

4.2. Listing fees in corporate bond markets

The listing fees associated with corporate bond issuance vary across markets. **In general, ten jurisdictions apply an initial listing fee, and six jurisdictions also charge an annual listing fee.** The initial listing fee is charged when corporate bonds are admitted to the market, and an annual fee is charged for each subsequent year of listing. Of the 11 jurisdictions with information available, only Chinese Taipei does not impose an initial listing fee. Of the other jurisdictions, six have a fixed initial listing fee, whereas four adjust the fee depending on the amount issued (Table 4.1). For example, in Australia, issuances below AUD 3 million incur a fee of AUD 45 000, with any amount exceeding this being subject to an additional proportional charge, and the proportion decreases as the base amount increases. In China, the fee is 0.01% of the issuance amount, with a minimum fee of RMB 5 000 and a maximum fee of RMB 20 000. An annual listing fee is charged in six jurisdictions, with five jurisdictions basing the annual listing fee on the issuance amount and only Japan charging a fixed annual fee. Five jurisdictions do not impose an annual listing fee. It is noteworthy that while Hong Kong (China) does not have an annual listing fee, the initial listing fee is determined by the maturity period for each corporate bond. This approach ensures that the fee structure takes into account the length of time the bonds will be listed on the stock exchange which could be considered equivalent to imposing an annual fee.

As an illustrative exercise, Table 4.2 compares the fees across different jurisdictions for bond issuances of USD 10 million and USD 50 million, both with a projected maturity of five years. Among the jurisdictions examined, only Australia has a listing fee surpassing 1% of the issuance amount. Korea has the lowest initial and annual listing fees with its maximum initial fee capped at KRW 1.7 million (approximately USD 1 316). China's fees are also competitive, for a bond issuance of USD 10 million, the fee is a mere 0.02% of the amount issued, and it is 0.04% for an issuance of USD 50 million.

Table 4.1. Corporate bond listing fee structure across selected markets

Jurisdiction	Initial listing fee	Annual listing fee
Australia	Regressive listing fee	Regressive annual listing fee
China	Proportional listing fee with lower and upper limits	Proportional annual listing fee with lower and upper limits
Hong Kong (China)	Regressive listing fee	No annual listing fee
India	Fixed listing fee	Regressive annual listing fee
Indonesia	Fixed listing fee	Regressive annual listing fee
Japan	Fixed listing fee	Fixed annual listing fee
Korea	Fixed listing fee	No annual listing fee
Malaysia	Fixed listing fee	No annual listing fee
Philippines	Regressive listing fee	No annual listing fee
Singapore	Fixed listing fee	No annual listing fee
Chinese Taipei	No listing fee	Proportional annual listing fee with upper limits

Note: Information for some jurisdictions was not available.
Source: Australian Stock Exchange, Shanghai Stock Exchange, Hong Kong Stock Exchange, National Stock Exchange of India, Indonesia Stock Exchange, Tokyo Stock Exchange, Korea Exchange, Bursa Malaysia, Philippine Stock Exchange, Singapore Exchange and Taiwan Stock Exchange.

Table 4.2. Corporate bond listing fees across selected markets (in USD)

Jurisdiction	Principle: USD 10 million				Principle: USD 50 million			
	Initial listing fee	Annual listing fee	Total (5 years)	As % of amount issued	Initial listing fee	Annual listing fee	Total (5 years)	As % of amount issued
Australia	62 594	20 923	167 210	1.67%	103 228	30 281	254 631	2.55%
China	1 000	148	1 742	0.02%	2 969	250	4 219	0.04%
Hong Kong (China)	2 554	-	2 554	0.03%	3 192	-	3 192	0.03%
India	636	3 817	19 719	0.20%	636	4 834	24 808	0.25%
Indonesia	1 684	2 500	14 184	0.14%	1 684	11 000	56 684	0.57%
Japan	7 605	760	11 407	0.11%	7 605	760	11 407	0.11%
Korea	774	77	1 161	0.01%	1 084	77	1 471	0.01%
Malaysia	3 408	-	3 408	0.03%	3 408	-	3 408	0.03%
Philippines	5 918	-	5 918	0.06%	25 918	-	25 918	0.26%
Singapore	18 133	-	18 133	0.18%	18 133	-	18 133	0.18%
Chinese Taipei	-	3 000	15 000	0.15%	-	15 000	75 000	0.75%

Note: Corporate bonds are presumed to be listed under the Standard/Regulated Tier of each market, with an assumed maturity of five years.
Source: Australian Stock Exchange, Shanghai Stock Exchange, Hong Kong Stock Exchange, National Stock Exchange of India, Indonesia Stock Exchange, Tokyo Stock Exchange, Korea Exchange, Bursa Malaysia, Philippine Stock Exchange, Singapore Exchange and Taiwan Stock Exchange.

4.3. Derivative markets

A well-functioning derivative market plays an important role by allowing investors to manage the risks associated with investments in corporate bonds. For instance, foreign investors can use currency derivatives to hedge their exposure to corporate bonds denominated in local currency. Moreover, credit default swaps (CDS) enable further investors to manage default risks (IMF, 2004[6]).

Thirteen jurisdictions have a functioning derivative market available to help manage risks associated with corporate bond investment (Figure 4.2, Panel A). Both financial instruments for mitigating currency risk and interest rate risk are offered in the markets of 11 jurisdictions, while CDS are available only in seven jurisdictions (Figure 4.2, Panel B).

Figure 4.2. Derivatives market to manage risks associated with corporate bonds

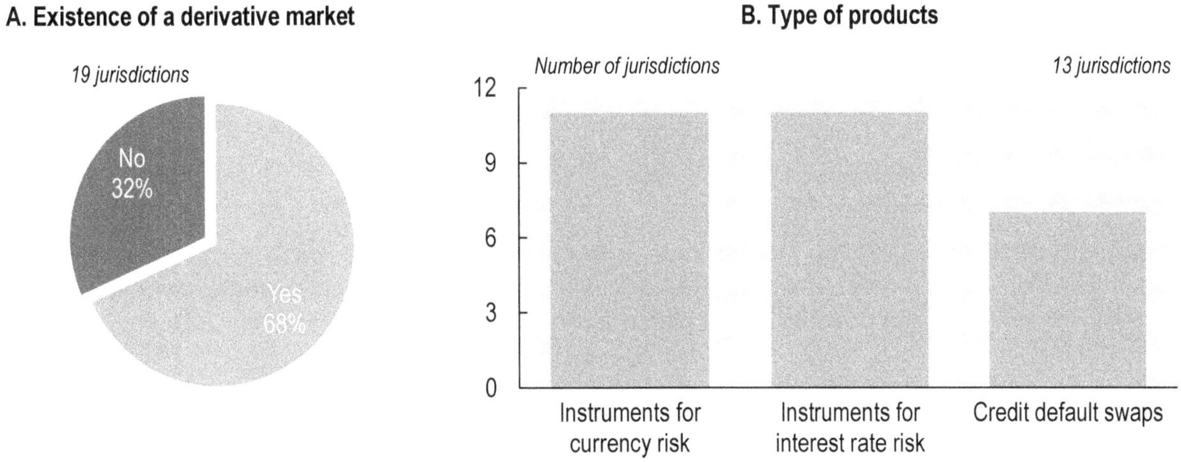

Source: OECD Survey on Access to Corporate Bond Markets for Growth Companies in Asia, see Annex B for details.

4.4. Market makers

Market makers contribute significantly to providing liquidity in capital markets and they could play important role, in particular, in underdeveloped corporate bond markets. **In 11 of the surveyed jurisdictions** (Australia, Bangladesh, China, Indonesia, Korea, Mongolia, Pakistan, Philippines, Singapore, Chinese Taipei and Viet Nam) **the legal or regulatory framework includes certain provisions regarding market making activities** (Figure 4.3, Panel A). Despite the presence of such provisions, market makers in these jurisdictions tend not to be very active. In fact, regulators in over half of the jurisdictions with market making provisions (Australia, Bangladesh, Indonesia, Korea, Mongolia and Pakistan) acknowledge that the market makers are not active in their corporate bond markets. For instance, in the Philippines, although registration of at least one market maker is included in the listing requirement for corporate bonds, market makers are not active. While market making activities are potentially profitable, such provisions tend to include financial incentives to further support their activities. In Korea, for instance, market makers are exempted from trading fees and the stock change will provide financial incentives depending on their market making performance (Korea Exchange, 2015[7]).

Figure 4.3. Market making activities

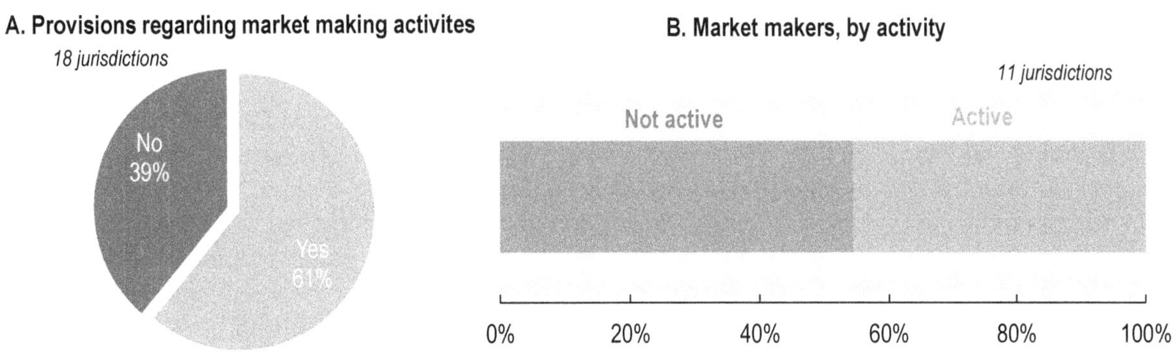

Source: OECD Survey on Access to Corporate Bond Markets for Growth Companies in Asia, see Annex B for details.

4.5. Government bond markets

The development of government bond markets generally improves the financial intermediation capacity of a market by establishing the required informational, legal and financial infrastructure. This enables the introduction of new financial products, including money market instruments, derivates and more importantly corporate bonds. At the same time, well-functioning corporate bond markets require a liquid benchmark local currency government bond yield curve. A domestic risk-free yield curve allows the pricing of risky securities, including corporate bonds.

Fifteen jurisdictions responded already have a well-established local currency government bond market whereas in Bangladesh, Cambodia, Mongolia and Pakistan, the local currency government bond market is still immature and currently developing (Figure 4.4).

Figure 4.4. Existence of a local currency government bond market

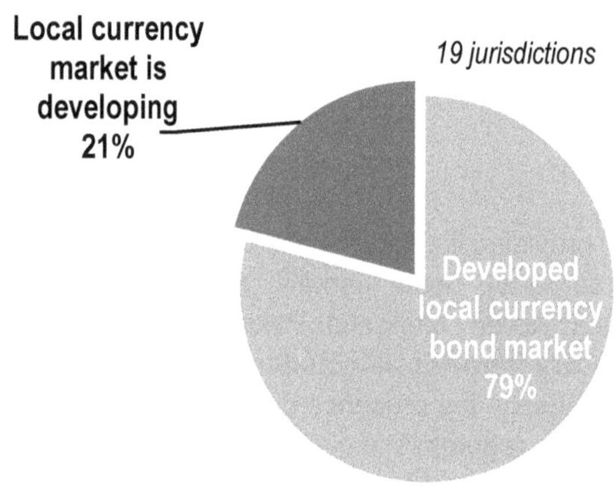

Source: OECD Survey on Access to Corporate Bond Markets for Growth Companies in Asia, see Annex B for details.

Significant differences exist across jurisdictions when assessing the size of the government bond market (measured by the general government bond debt-to-GDP ratios) (Figure 4.5). In the region, Japan has the highest ratio of general government bond debt-to-GDP (261%). In six jurisdictions, the general government bond debt represented less than 50% of their respective GDP in 2022: Indonesia (40%), Bangladesh (39%), Cambodia (37%), Viet Nam (37%), Chinese Taipei (27%) and Hong Kong (China) (4%). In terms of outstanding amounts, China has the largest market for government bonds with almost USD 14 trillion, followed by Japan and India with outstanding amount of USD 11 trillion and almost USD 3 trillion, respectively. In the rest of jurisdictions, the size of the government bond market is less than USD 1 trillion.

The government bond market is in its very early stages of development in Bangladesh, Cambodia, Mongolia and Pakistan. Lao PDR despite not stating the non-existence of a local currency bond market has only active bonds denominated in non-domestic currency. Currently, Mongolia does not have a local currency government bond market, and until September 2022, Cambodia did not either. Some of the important components of a well-developed government bond market include extending the yield curve, setting up issuance calendars to improve transparency, increasing the disclosure of information on public debt issuance and statistics, holding regular meetings with dealers, institutional investors and rating agencies, introducing a system of primary dealers, and establishing a repurchase (repo) market in the government bond market.

In Asia, governments can borrow with maturities ranging from 15 years in Sri Lanka to 50 years in Korea and Singapore. The average maturity for the outstanding debt stock (where available) ranges between 6.7 years in Singapore to 11.9 years in India (Figure 4.5). Extending government debt maturities can mitigate refinancing risks, stabilise funding costs, and enhance investor confidence, fostering long-term fiscal planning. Additionally, the longest maturity in the yield curve serves as a crucial benchmark, influencing various financial instruments and providing insights into long-term market expectations and economic conditions. While the longest maturity may not necessarily indicate the level of market development, well-established government markets often have the capacity to issue longer maturities.

While credit ratings for domestic long-term government borrowing provide insights into the creditworthiness of a government and could include assessment of certain factors related to the level of the development of the market, they alone may not fully capture the overall development of government bond markets. Figure 4.5 provides information on the most recent rating for domestic long-term government debt, except for Cambodia, where the rating pertains to foreign currency long-term government debt. **The majority of jurisdictions have an investment grade rating,** except Bangladesh, Cambodia, Mongolia, Lao PDR, Pakistan, Sri Lanka and Viet Nam.

Figure 4.5. Overview of government bond markets in selected jurisdictions in 2022

	% of GDP	Amount outstanding (USD billions)	Longest maturity of government bonds (years)	Average maturity of outstanding stock (years)	Credit rating
Japan	261%	11 062	40	9	A
Singapore	134%	626	50	6.7	AAA
Lao PDR	129%	20	-	-	CCC
Sri Lanka	118%	89	15	-	CCC
India	83%	2 815	40	11.9	BBB
Mongolia	82%	14	-	-	B
China	77%	13 955	30	8.5	A
Pakistan	76%	285	20	-	B
Malaysia	66%	270	30	9.5	A
Thailand	61%	325	50	10.3	A
Philippines	58%	233	20	-	A
Australia	56%	948	30	7	AAA
Korea	54%	905	50	11.7	AA
Indonesia	40%	527	30	8.1	BBB
Bangladesh	39%	180	20	6.9	B
Viet Nam	37%	151	30	9.2	BB
Cambodia	37%	10	-	-	B
Chinese Taipei	27%	209	30	-	AA
Hong Kong (China)	4%	15	20	-	AA

Note: Credit rating refers to the most recent rating displayed on the LSEG Issuer Ratings' screen for domestic long-term government debt, except for Cambodia, where the rating pertains to foreign currency long-term government debt. The average maturity of outstanding stock information is based on the latest available data. Specifically, for Japan, India, Malaysia, Australia and Indonesia, data is provided for the year 2023. For Korea and Viet Nam data refers to 2021, while for Bangladesh, data refers to 2020, for Singapore and Thailand data refers to 2019.
Source: IMF World Economic Outlook Database, LSEG.

The most developed markets in Asia have measures in place to improve the transparency and promotion of government bond markets. For example, the Australian Office of Financial Management (AOFM) employs various means to engage with financial markets. Weekly announcements provide details on upcoming transactions, while broader guidance on issuance plans, including annual volumes and the introduction of new bond lines, is disseminated a few times annually. Additionally, the release of weekly notices for forthcoming transactions maintained a consistent schedule, ensuring predictability, and all tenders and syndications were conducted in accordance with the information provided in those notices (AOFM, 2023[8]). Likewise, in Japan, following established debt management policies, the government carefully communicates with the market through various meetings for the formulation and operation of the issuance plan. The aim is to align issuance closely with market requirements and address the diversification of bondholders (MOF Japan, 2023[9]). Additionally, Japan, has a system of primary dealers to ensure secure and stable issuance, while sustaining and enhancing liquidity in government bond markets. This system grants specific privileges to select auction participants who undertake essential responsibilities aligned with debt management policies (MOF Japan, 2023[10]). In Korea, the financial market hosts various government bond-related markets, including the repo market, STRIPS,[3] futures, and ETFs, which have been introduced by the Korean government to contribute to the overall promotion and enhancement of the primary government bond market and the broader market ecosystem (Korean Ministry of Economy and Finance, 2021[11]).

4.6. Research on growth companies

The availability of research on companies issuing securities can facilitate the development of corporate bond markets by providing investors with information on companies and therefore supporting informed trading. This is particularly important for growth companies as they often lack analyst coverage that could introduce these companies to the market and keep investors updated. To mitigate the information gaps between growth companies and investors, jurisdictions in many parts of the world, including Asia, have introduced measures to provide research coverage for smaller companies. For example, in Europe, the Hungary's stock exchange subsidises the research activity of brokerage companies. Furthermore, in Romania, the Bucharest Stock Exchange developed a programme called BVB Research Hub, with the purpose of facilitating research coverage for small and mid-cap companies (OECD, 2022[12]).

More than half of the jurisdictions (Australia, China, Hong Kong (China), India, Indonesia, Japan, Lao PDR, Malaysia, Chinese Taipei and Viet Nam) **have an institution or intermediary that provides research on growth companies** (Figure 4.6, Panel A).

Figure 4.6. Research coverage on growth companies

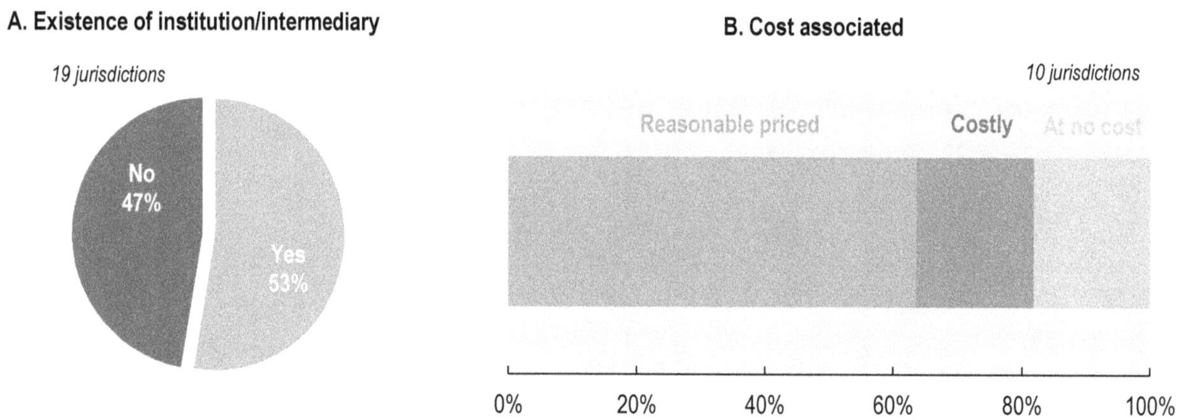

Source: OECD Survey on Access to Corporate Bond Markets for Growth Companies in Asia, see Annex B for details.

In 80% of the jurisdictions having an institution in charge of providing research on growth companies, investors are able to access this information at no cost or at a reasonable price. The cost of this research can represent a barrier to accessing such information. In Asia, investors in Australia and Indonesia can access some information on growth companies at no cost, while it is perceived as costly in Lao PDR and Viet Nam (Figure 4.6, Panel B). In Australia, China, Hong Kong (China), India, Japan, Malaysia and Chinese Taipei, investors are able to access some research on growth companies at a reasonable price. In particular, in Indonesia, all market participants can access data about SMEs as it is provided at no cost by the Ministry of Cooperatives and SMEs. Malaysia implemented a research programme on SMEs via governmental agencies (Malaysia External Trade Development Corporation and SME Corporation Malaysia) to accelerate the reputation and credibility of growth companies.

References

AOFM (2023), *Australian Office of Financial Management - Annual Report 2022-23*, [8]
https://www.aofm.gov.au/sites/default/files/2023-10-19/AOFM%202022-23%20Annual%20Report_WEB.pdf.

ICMA (2022), *ICMA Bond Market Transparency Directory*, https://www.icmagroup.org/market-practice-and-regulatory-policy/secondary-markets/market-transparency/global-overview-of-bond-market-post-trade-transparency-regimes/. [3]

IMF (2004), *Emerging Local Securities and Derivatives Markets*, International Monetary Fund, [6]
https://doi.org/10.5089/9781589062917.083.

JSDA (2019), *Rules Concerning Publication of Over-the-Counter Trading Reference Prices, etc. and Trading Prices of Bonds*, https://www.jsda.or.jp/en/rules-guidelines/E45.pdf. [5]

Korea Exchange (2015), *KRX BondsALL*, [7]
https://global.krx.co.kr/contents/GLB/06/0604/0604010100/GLB0604010100.jsp#d3f4f32f89474168cc558d9631a5d5a0=5.

Korean Ministry of Economy and Finance (2021), *Korea Treasury Bonds*, [11]
https://ktb.moef.go.kr/eng/publications.do.

MOF Japan (2023), *Debt Management Report 2023*, [9]
https://www.mof.go.jp/english/policy/jgbs/publication/debt_management_report/2023/esaimu2023.pdf.

MOF Japan (2023), *JGB Market Special Participants Scheme*, [10]
https://www.mof.go.jp/english/policy/jgbs/debt_management/pd/index.html (accessed on November 2023).

OECD (2022), *Capital Market Review of Romania: Towards a National Strategy*, OECD Publishing, Paris, https://doi.org/10.1787/9bfc0339-en. [12]

OJK (2020), *Regulation No. 20/POJK.04/2020 Concerning Trustee Contracts for Debt Securities and/or Sukuk*, https://ojk.go.id/id/regulasi/Documents/Pages/Kontrak-Perwaliamanatan-Efek-Bersifat-Utang-dan-atau-Sukuk--/POJK%2020-2020.pdf#search=20%2FPOJK%2E04%2F2020. [1]

OJK (2020), *Regulation No. 57 /POJK.04/2020 Offering securities through technology-based crowdfunding services*, https://ojk.go.id/id/regulasi/Documents/Pages/Penawaran-Efek-Melalui-Layanan-Urun-Dana-Berbasis-Teknologi-Informasi/pojk%2057%20-%2004%20-%202020.pdf#search=No%2E%2020%2FPOJK%2E04%2F2020. [2]

OJK (2015), *Regulation X.M.3 Reports of Securities Transaction Decision of the Chairman of the Capital Market and Fiancial Institutions Supervisory Agency Number: KEP - 123/BL/2009 Concerning Reports of Securities Transaction*, https://ojk.go.id/en/kanal/pasar-modal/regulasi/klasifikasi-bapepam/peraturan-lainnya/Documents/01TerjemahanPeraturanXM3_1420162665.pdf. [4]

Notes

[1] Out of the 18 jurisdictions providing information in this chapter.

[2] The eligibility for using securities crowdfunding is restricted to companies that meet the following criteria: i) a legal entity independent of another legal entity; ii) a non-public company; and iii) a legal entity with net worth less than IDR 10 billion (c. USD 645 thousand).

[3] A financial instrument that separates the principal and interest of bonds and enables trading of them as marketable securities.

5 Credit ratings and bondholder rights in Asia

This chapter focusses on credit risk assessment of corporate bond issuers and bondholder rights, benefiting from the insights of the OECD Survey conducted among 19 regulators from 18 Asian jurisdictions and Australia. It addresses topics including the existence of credit rating agencies and alternative credit rating systems, as well as the requirements related to credit ratings for issuing corporate bonds. It also examines various aspects supporting the protection of bondholder rights such as trustee requirements, insolvency frameworks, covenants in corporate bond contracts and the presence of industry associations.

5.1. Credit ratings

Credit ratings play a crucial role in corporate bond markets by providing investors an opinion about the creditworthiness of the issuer. Credit rating agencies generally analyse available information to assess the credit risk, presenting their findings in an accessible and understandable format for use by market professionals. Since not all issuers target the same type of investors, international CRAs play a role to help domestic issuers in accessing global capital markets, while domestic CRAs usually focus on addressing the needs of domestic investors. In general, easy and affordable access to rating agencies and familiarity with the rating process significantly increases companies' ability to use long-term debt securities (Çelik, Demirtaş and Isaksson, 2020[1]). The OECD Survey explores several aspects of the credit rating systems available in Asia.

All jurisdictions have registered at least one or more credit rating agencies (CRAs) (Figure 5.1, Panel A). Results from the survey also indicate that the CRAs operating in nine jurisdictions[1] are domestic CRAs, while international CRAs and regional CRAs operate in a small number of jurisdictions. Both domestic and international CRAs[2] are operating in Australia, Chinese Taipei and Viet Nam. International CRAs operate only in Hong Kong (China) and Singapore, and only a regional CRA is used in Lao PDR. China, India and Thailand have domestic, regional and international CRAs operating in their markets. International CRAs operate in ten jurisdictions.[3]

Obtaining a credit rating for a bond issuance from CRAs can be unaffordable for smaller issuers which could impede their access to corporate bond financing. To address this issue and support market-based financing for smaller companies, some jurisdictions have introduced alternative credit rating systems where an institution other than a CRA provides rating services. Outside Asia, some markets have established alternative rating systems. In France, the Banque de France provides a credit score for individual firms for a fee, through the FIBEN (Fichier bancaire des entreprises) system.[4]

In Asia, alternative credit rating systems have been adopted only in three jurisdictions (Hong Kong (China), Korea and Malaysia) (Figure 5.1, Panel B). In Korea, the collateralised bond obligations guarantee scheme introduced by the Korea Credit Guarantee Fund (KODIT) uses an internal credit rating system to evaluate the credit risk of non-financial corporations to facilitate financing at a lower cost and allow institutional investors to purchase high-credit quality bonds. KODIT has developed three credit risk assessment models to assess the credit risk of credit guarantees granted to corporations. The Corporate Credit Rating System (CCRS) evaluates the credit risk of companies with total assets over KRW 1 billion. The Small Enterprise Scoring System (SESS) and the Start-up Business Scoring System (SBSS) assess the credit risk of SMEs and start-up companies respectively (KODIT, 2019[2]).[5]

Similarly, in Malaysia, the SME Corporation Malaysia[6] is a government agency that co-ordinates the implementation of development programmes for SMEs across all related ministries and agencies. It acts as the central point of reference for research and data dissemination on SMEs and entrepreneurs, as well as providing business advisory services for SMEs and entrepreneurs throughout Malaysia. It also offers an SME Competitiveness Rating for Enhancement (SCORE). SCORE is a diagnostic tool used to rate and enhance the competitiveness of SMEs based on their performance and capabilities. SCORE has also been used as a business matching tool for better market access, as well as an initial indicator for the purposes of access to finance.[7]

The alternative credit scoring system in Hong Kong (China) is designed to allow SMEs to access bank financing (Hong Kong Monetary Authority, 2020[3]). This alternative credit scoring offers banks the ability to expand the range of data that they use to assess an entity's creditworthiness. Whereas conventional credit scoring uses a limited range of financial data, the alternative credit scoring takes advantage of new technology to obtain and use alternative data that can provide valuable insights about an entity's creditworthiness. This alternative data may include information about, for example, an entity's trade payments, sales transaction records, credit analysis reports and the behavioural characteristics of its business executives.

Figure 5.1. Existence Credit Rating Agencies by type, and alternative credit rating systems

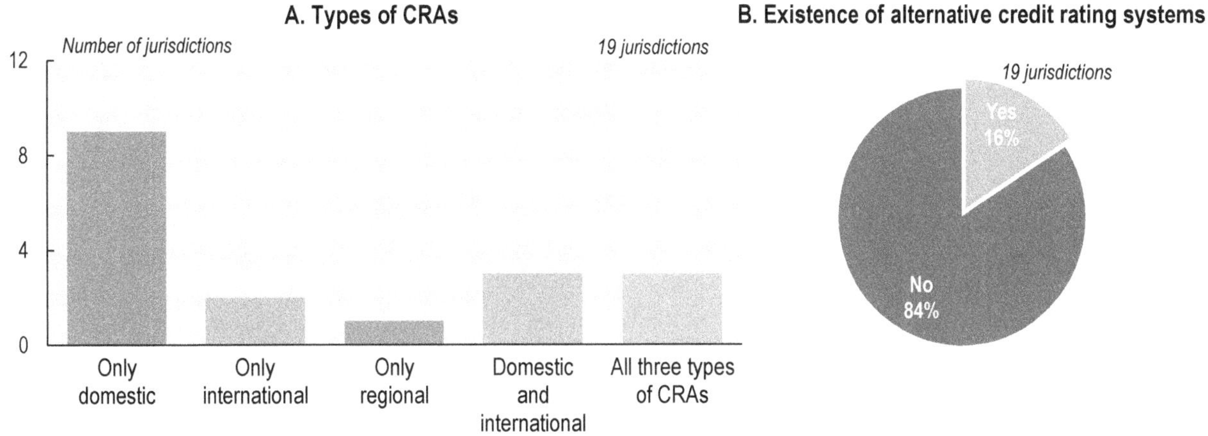

Source: OECD Survey on Access to Corporate Bond Markets for Growth Companies in Asia, see Annex B for details.

Having international CRAs operating in the domestic markets could contribute to the accuracy of the overall rating process and could indirectly enhance the development and expansion of domestic CRAs in Asia. Additional information provided by the surveyed jurisdictions indicate that both in Malaysia and Bangladesh some of the domestic CRAs are affiliated with international CRAs through their stakes in domestic CRAs. For example, in Malaysia, Moody's Asia Pacific Limited owns 19.5% of Malaysian Rating Corporation Berhad (MARC, a domestic CRA) while S&P Global Asian Holdings Pte Ltd. owns 19.2% of Rating Services Berhad (RAM Ratings, a domestic CRA).

IOSCO provides guidance in its Code of Conduct Fundamentals for Credit Rating Agencies considering possible challenges with CRA systems and decision-making process (IOSCO, 2015[4]). Also, national authorities in certain jurisdictions have adopted regulations to ensure sound regulatory practices and governance of CRAs. For example, European regulation[8] prevents authorities from interfering in the content of credit ratings or in their methodologies. In the United States,[9] the Securities and Exchange Commission is not allowed to interfere in the content of credit ratings nor the procedures and methodologies. In Asia, similar frameworks have been established in Australia, Hong Kong (China) and Singapore amongst others.

With the aim of improving rating quality through mutual co-operation among domestic CRAs in the region, the Association of Credit Rating Agencies in Asia (ACRAA) was established in 2001. ACRAA addresses issues relating credit ratings by promoting best practices, offering joint training and collecting global regulatory information. Since then, 28 members have joined the ACRAA initiative from 15 Asian jurisdictions. Table 5.1 shows the 2023 list of domestic CRA members of ACRAA. China and India have the highest number of domestic CRAs that are members of ACRAA (five), followed by Bangladesh (four), Malaysia and Pakistan (two each). In other jurisdictions, there is only one domestic CRA that is affiliated with ACRAA.

Table 5.1. Number of domestic CRAs members of ACRAA in 2023

Jurisdiction	Number of domestic CRAs	Jurisdiction	Number of domestic CRAs
Bangladesh	4	Malaysia	2
China	5	Pakistan	2
India	5	Philippines	1
Indonesia	1	Chinese Taipei	1
Japan	1	Thailand	1
Korea	1	Viet Nam	1

Note: Please be aware that CRAs not registered with ACRAA may not appear in this list as is the case with Thailand that has an additional domestic CRA.
Source: (Japan Credit Rating Agency, Ltd, 2023[5]).

As a comparison, in Europe, domestic and regional CRAs also play an important role in some markets as the current European regulation requires credit rating agencies to be certified or registered with the European Securities and Markets Authority (ESMA) to rate a European bond issuer. A total of 30 rating agencies have registered with ESMA and three are registered in non-European countries, specifically, in Japan, Mexico and the United States. Germany has the largest number of domestic CRAs (five), followed by Italy (three), Spain (two) and Ireland (one). In seven European jurisdictions, these rating agencies have affiliations to internationally recognised CRAs (Table 5.2).

Table 5.2. CRAs certified to operate in Europe with affiliations to internationally recognised CRAs

Jurisdiction	Number of subsidiaries of internationally recognised CRAs	Name of internationally recognised CRAs	Number of other domestic or regional CRAs
France	1	Moody's	-
Germany	1	Moody's	5
Ireland	2	Fitch Ratings	1
		S&P Global Ratings	
Italy	1	Moody's	3
Spain	1	Moody's	2
Sweden	1	Moody's	-

Note: Internationally recognised CRAs refer to three agencies: Fitch Ratings, Moody's and S&P Global Ratings. The statistics have been compiled using information available on ESMA's website as of 23 March 2023. This table only shows jurisdictions where subsidiaries of internationally recognised CRAs are established in addition to domestic or regional CRAs.
Source: (ESMA, 2024[6])

Credit ratings also play an increasingly important role in the corporate bond market by influencing the investment decisions and asset allocation of financial and non-financial institutions in a number of different ways. One of them is through regulations that impose quantitative limits on holdings of corporate bonds such as risk-based capital requirements. Credit ratings are also used extensively in investment choices through self-defined investment policies by investors who focus exclusively or primarily on buying investment grade bonds. Moreover, many bond investment funds are also bound by rating-based indexes and investment mandates that are defined with reference to ratings. Importantly, cross-border investments in corporate bonds, which now constitute a significant share of the global market, are also likely to depend on rating- or index-based strategies (Çelik, Demirtaş and Isaksson, 2020[1]).

A credit rating is required to issue a corporate bond in 12 jurisdictions (Bangladesh, Cambodia, India, Indonesia, Korea, Lao PDR, Malaysia, Mongolia, Pakistan, Philippines, Sri Lanka and Thailand; Figure 5.2, Panel A). Additionally, within jurisdictions where ratings are required for bond issuance, at least one rating is required in 80% of the jurisdictions and two ratings are required in two jurisdictions (Bangladesh and Korea) (Figure 5.2, Panel B). For example, in Korea, most corporate bonds are issued without guarantee and where a financial investment company underwrites these bonds credit assessment from two or more CRAs is required (ADB, 2018[7]).

Four jurisdictions require an investment grade rating for corporate bonds (Bangladesh, Indonesia, Pakistan and Sri Lanka) **and a minimum level for credit rating other than an investment grade rating is required in seven jurisdictions** (Cambodia, India, Korea, Lao PDR, Malaysia, Philippines and Thailand) (Figure 5.2, Panel B). For instance, detailed information provided by the survey respondents suggests that no credit rating is required in the case of unlisted privately placed bonds in Pakistan and one notch above investment grade rating is required for corporate bond issuance in Sri Lanka. In Bangladesh, for private placement, a minimum BBB rating in the long-term is required. Similarly, a minimum A rating in the long-term is required for public issues. In Indonesia, securities that can be issued through a continuous public offering of debt securities and/or sukuk have a rating that is included in the top four categories based on the Securities Rating Companies' rating classification.

Figure 5.2. Requirements related to credit ratings to issue corporate bonds

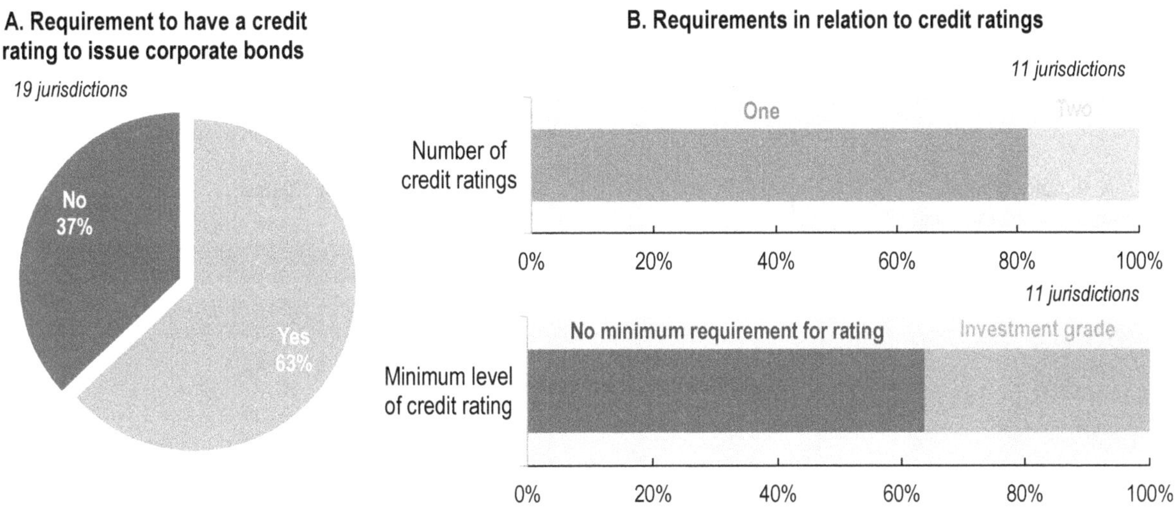

Source: OECD Survey on Access to Corporate Bond Markets for Growth Companies in Asia, see Annex B for details.

5.2. Bondholder rights

Important characteristics differentiate corporate bondholders from other creditors, especially banks. Corporate bondholders tend to be more dispersed than other creditors. This results in challenges related to monitoring and co-ordination, for example making it more difficult for bondholders to take action when issues arise. In addition, the existence of intermediaries such as custodians could pose a challenge for bondholders and issuers to. During insolvency procedures this can be problematic because the company may have to undertake a process to ask bondholders to identify themselves (de Oliveira, Magnusson and Mulazimoglu, 2022[8]; Brodie, 2017[9]).

The OECD Survey investigated different aspects supporting the protection of bondholder rights in 18 Asian jurisdictions and Australia, including trustee requirements, insolvency frameworks, covenants in corporate bond contracts and the existence of industry associations.

5.2.1. Role of the trustee

In corporate bond markets, trustees play one of the most important roles in protecting the rights of bondholders. The specifics of how the trustee performs its duties will vary depending on each bond contract and the framework in each jurisdiction. However, there are often few incentives for trustees to act early to protect bondholder rights. This can be attributed to their fixed fee structure (typically paid by the issuer) and the varying obligations of trustees, with some not having a mandate to actively monitor until a covenant breach occurs. Trustees will need to be indemnified and instructed to act in many circumstances, which will depend on the specific facts. The annual fixed fee for the trustee does not take into account the additional work that is involved or the potential liability of the trustee taking action on behalf of the bondholders. In relation to their monitoring role, a trustee is usually provided with an annual compliance certificate/report in relation to the covenants of the bond contract drafted by the issuer. However, this is usually a simple compliance statement, and the trustee may not have to take active steps to assess whether the report is accurate (de Oliveira, Magnusson and Mulazimoglu, 2022[8]). In a number of Asian markets, it is also common for non-trustee fiscal agent structures to be present.

In 14 of jurisdictions (Australia, Bangladesh, China, India, Indonesia, Japan, Lao PDR, Malaysia, Pakistan, Philippines, Singapore, Sri Lanka, Chinese Taipei and Thailand) **the legal or regulatory framework requires the appointment of a trustee for corporate bond issuances** (Figure 5.3, Panel A). In all jurisdictions, the trustee is required to be appointed by the issuer. In two jurisdictions (Hong Kong (China) and Mongolia), while the legal or regulatory framework does not require the appointment of a trustee, it is a market practice for an issuer to appoint a trustee. In 17 of the 19 jurisdictions, the trustee is paid by the issuer.

Figure 5.3. Provisions for appointment of a trustee and its role in regulatory frameworks

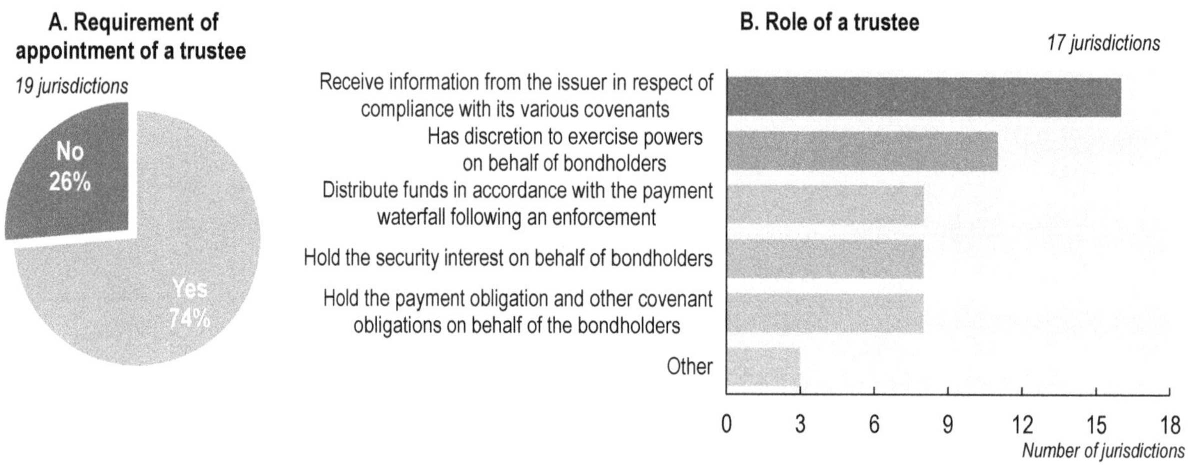

Source: OECD Survey on Access to Corporate Bond Markets for Growth Companies in Asia, see Annex B for details.

In Singapore, the details about who pays the trustee are not prescribed in the legal or regulatory framework, but rather it depends on what is specified in the trust deed. In Indonesia, only when it comes to large-company bonds, the legal and regulatory framework requires the issuer to appoint the trustee. Under OJK regulations, although the trustee represents the interests of holders of debt securities and/or sukuk, the trustee contract is stipulated to be an agreement between the issuer and the trustee specifically for the issuance of debt securities and/or sukuk. The trustee requirement does not apply to securities crowdfunding used by SMEs where financing is raised directly from investors through an open securities crowdfunding platform. In this case, the relevant framework was provided by an OJK regulation, which aimed to provide alternative funding for SMEs, as well as business start-ups to obtain funds through the capital market, by expanding the scope of securities offerings in crowdfunding services (OJK, 2020[10]; 2020[11]; Government of Indonesia, 2023[12]).

In the 19 jurisdictions surveyed, trustees play a range of core roles, as shown in Figure 5.3 (Panel B). The primary role of the trustee is to receive information from the issuer regarding compliance with its various covenants (16 jurisdictions). This is followed by the trustee having the discretion to act on behalf of bondholders, for example when there is a declaration of a default event, when bond covenants are triggered, among other events (11 jurisdictions). Other less common roles are: distributing funds in accordance with the payment waterfall following an enforcement (8 jurisdictions); holding the security interest on behalf of bondholders (8 jurisdictions); and holding the payment obligation and other covenant obligations on behalf of the bondholders (3 jurisdictions).

One of the examples of these trustee roles is from Bangladesh, where the trustee of a debt security only bears the legal/regulatory obligations on behalf of bondholders and the trustee is not bound by financial obligations. In Indonesia, new regulation aims at strengthening the independence, objectivity and professionalism of the trustee in carrying out their duties (OJK, 2020[10]).

Three jurisdictions (Malaysia, Singapore and Chinese Taipei) **responded that there were other roles for the trustee**. In Malaysia, the specific duties and powers of the trustee are specified in the law and guidelines (Government of Malaysia, 2007[13]; SC Malaysia, 2020[14]). Among the duties of the trustee in Malaysia are the following: it must be satisfied that information disclosed in relation to the bond is not inconsistent with the terms, provisions and covenants; ensures the borrower complies with the Malaysian Companies Act; takes reasonable steps to ensure that the borrower remedies a covenant breach; notifies the Securities Commission if a breach is not remedied by the borrower and call a meeting of bondholders; present proposals to protect bondholder interests and obtain their directions. In addition, Chapter 19 of the Malaysian Securities Commissions Guidelines on Trust Deeds specifies powers and duties of the trustee. For example, the trust deed must require the trustee to use a reasonable degree of skill and diligence in exercising their rights and powers in the event of default or enforcement and to notify credit rating agencies about material events where corporate bonds or sukuk are rated.

In Chinese Taipei, the Company Act sets out other the role of the trustees, which includes: receiving the complete list of bondholders prepared by the board of directors; checking and supervising the performance by the company in relation to the obligations associated with corporate bonds, for the interest of bondholders; convening meetings of corporate bondholders for matters concerning the common interest of corporate bondholders; and executing the resolutions adopted at the meeting of corporate bondholders (Gorvernment of Chinese Taipei, 2021[15]). In Singapore, the Securities and Futures Act 2001 requires trustees to exercise due diligence and vigilance in carrying out their functions and duties, and in safeguarding the rights and interests of bondholders.

5.2.2. Insolvency frameworks

While approaches may differ, effective corporate insolvency frameworks share common objectives. One of the main objectives is to promote the reorganisation of viable but financially distressed firms, and also to facilitate the reallocation of assets of non-viable businesses (World Bank, 2016[16]). The existence of effective and efficient insolvency frameworks in the markets is also recognised by the G20/OECD Principles on Corporate Governance, "[t]he corporate governance framework should be complemented by an effective and efficient insolvency framework and by effective enforcement of creditor rights" (OECD, 2023[17]).

Studies have demonstrated that effective insolvency systems are associated with an increase in the general availability and cost of credit, and a higher recovery rate for creditors (World Bank, 2014[18]). Functioning insolvency laws that govern formal procedures for financially distressed companies are required prior to formal bankruptcy procedures. Importantly, the performance of an insolvency framework is greatly dependent on the efficiency of the judicial system within which it operates (OECD, 2021[19]).

Fourteen jurisdictions include provisions for "negotiation to occur between bondholders and bond issuers" (Figure 5.4, Panel A). While negotiations can occur at any time and in any jurisdiction, the negotiations referred in this report relate to situations where there are provisions outlined in the legal or regulatory frameworks. For example, in the Philippines, the law provides for pre-negotiated rehabilitation, which aims to help companies that are insolvent or may become insolvent. This option is generally available only where the company can show creditors that the recovery will be higher if the company continues as a going concern rather than being liquidated quickly (Government of the Philippines, 2010[20]; Clifford Chance, 2018[21]).

In addition, 13 jurisdictions have provisions in their insolvency frameworks that allow "firms to initiate insolvency proceedings before becoming insolvent" (Figure 5.4, Panel A). It is important to note that insolvency proceedings comprise both reorganisation and liquidation procedures. For example, in Australia, under the Corporations Act 2001, the company has the option in certain circumstances, to commence a voluntary winding up of a company when the company is solvent. This does not require a court sanction (Government of Australia, 2001[22]).

Figure 5.4. Insolvency systems

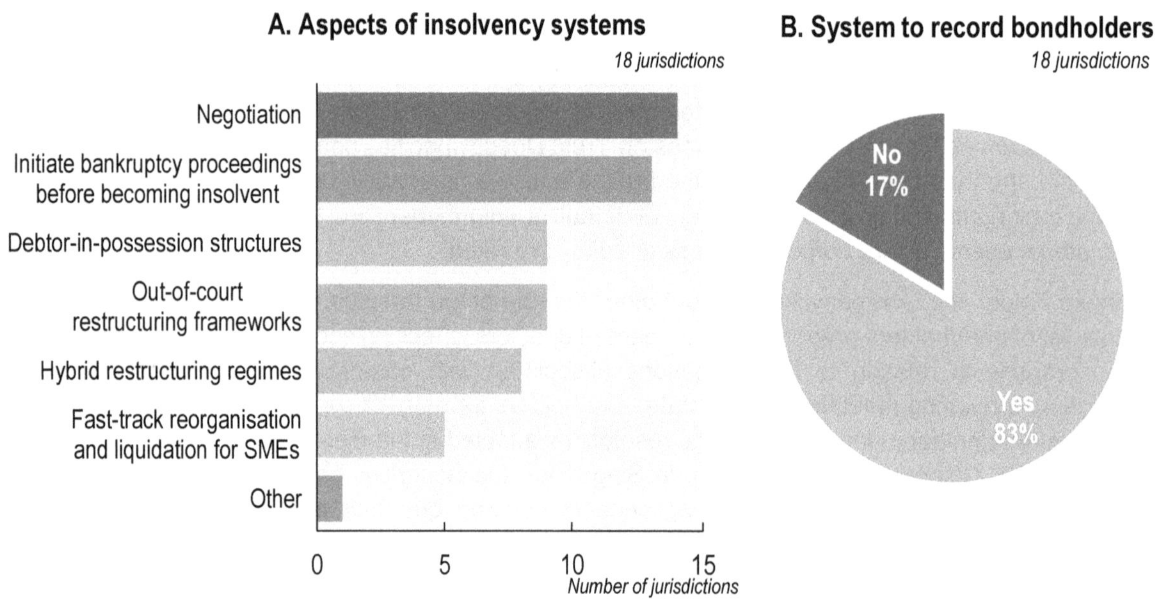

Source: OECD Survey on Access to Corporate Bond Markets for Growth Companies in Asia, see Annex B for details.

Nine jurisdictions have a "debtor-in-possession" style reorganisation procedures (Australia, Hong Kong (China), Japan, Korea, Philippines, Singapore, Chinese Taipei Thailand and Viet Nam) (Figure 5.4, Panel A). These structures allow management to continue running the company during the restructuring procedure. For example, in Japan, civil rehabilitation is the general debtor-in-possession reorganisation procedure. It is broadly similar to the Chapter 11 proceedings in the United States, which is sometimes referred to as reorganisation bankruptcy. While the civil rehabilitation procedure was initially introduced for SMEs in Japan, all types of companies and individuals can follow this procedure. The purpose of the Civil Rehabilitation Act is to form rehabilitation plans that are consented to by a number of creditors and confirmed by the court, to co-ordinate the various rights and obligations of debtors and creditors. Either the company or the creditors can apply to the court for civil rehabilitation if the required circumstances are met (Government of Japan, 1999[23]; Clifford Chance, 2018[21]; Nishimura & Asahi, 2011[24]).

"Out-of-court workouts/restructuring"[10] frameworks are present in the insolvency frameworks of nine jurisdictions (Australia, China, Hong Kong (China), Indonesia, Japan, Malaysia, Philippines, Sri Lanka and Viet Nam) (Figure 5.4, Panel A). An example of this restructuring is a distressed debt exchange, which is a way for a company in default to resolve its financial distress. A distressed debt exchange can be proposed by a company for several reasons, for instance, it may aim to: avoid a bankruptcy; improve liquidity; reduce debt; manage its maturity dates; and to reduce or eliminate onerous covenants. There are various benefits of distressed exchanges to corporations facing difficulties and their investors. Bankruptcy can be a lengthy and devaluing process, which can possibly be avoided by a distressed exchange. Creditors may accept a distressed debt exchange as they anticipate that the outcome may be worse for them under a bankruptcy (de Oliveira, Magnusson and Mulazimoglu, 2022[8]). It has been documented that distressed exchanges increase recovery rates compared to a bankruptcy situation (World Bank, 2014[18]), however unsuccessful distressed debt exchanges may mean that bankruptcy is more likely (Fitch Ratings, 2020[25]). Generally, distressed exchanges are offered to a specific subset of creditors, which can make the transaction easier.

Some jurisdictions have developed standardised out-of-court restructuring processes, which are centralised frameworks designed for large numbers of restructurings where the debtors have common characteristics (FSB, 2022[26]). In Philippines, the Financial Rehabilitation and Insolvency Act of 2010 recognises out-of-court restructuring agreements and rehabilitation plans to be analogous to a court sanctioned plan. There are several conditions for this to occur: firstly, the company must agree to it; and secondly, the plan must be approved by creditors who hold at least 85% of the total liabilities of the company. The plan must be published for several weeks in a newspaper of general circulation in Philippines (Government of the Philippines, 2010[20]; Clifford Chance, 2018[21]). Korea has already included certain out-of-court restructuring procedures in their insolvency system. In an aim to improve the procedures, the revised version of the insolvency regime enacted in 2001 included shorter deadlines, allowed debtor-in-possession structures and permitted shareholders to repurchase converted equity (Bergthaler et al., 2015[27]).

"Hybrid restructuring regimes" are provided for in the insolvency frameworks of 8 jurisdictions (Hong Kong (China), India, Korea, Lao PDR, Malaysia, Singapore, Sri Lanka and Viet Nam) (Figure 5.4, Panel A). These hybrid regimes are informal workout procedures that combine contractual workouts with limited court intervention. They may involve "[s]ome formal legal elements (e.g. stay on assets, cram downs), but negotiations are primarily conducted directly between debtor and creditor(s) without court involvement" (de Oliveira, Magnusson and Mulazimoglu, 2022[8]). Hybrid restructuring mechanisms can be a preferred option in times of economic crisis, as they do not solely rely on court processes which may be under pressure. Research has shown that "[h]ybrid restructuring provides an effective way of dealing with hold-out creditors, since it may involve the limited intervention of the courts with the effect of blocking creditor actions (stay of creditor actions) or imposing a restructuring plan adopted by a majority (binding the dissenting creditor minority)" (Dutra Araujo et al., 2022[28]).

A small number of jurisdictions (Australia, India, Singapore and Viet Nam) have a specialised growth company or SME bankruptcy regime to fast-track reorganisation and liquidation for these companies (Figure 5.4, Panel A). These streamlined processes can help firms to exit the mark and prevent the accumulation of "zombie firms" (World Bank Group, 2021[29]). For example, the Australian government introduced small business-specific amendments to the insolvency laws to mitigate impacts of the COVID-19 pandemic. The amendments permit a liquidator to use a new small business liquidation process, instead of the general creditor's voluntary liquidation process, to expedite the creditor's voluntary winding up process. The amendments also provide a debt restructuring process for eligible small companies (Government of Australia, 2001[22]; 2020[30]). In Singapore, the Insolvency, Restructuring and Dissolution Act 1998 was amended in 2020 and came into effect in 2021 to create a Simplified Insolvency Programme (Government of Singapore, 2018[31]). The act states that the aim is to provide "a simplified process for the restructuring of debts to any eligible company that seeks to enter into a compromise or an arrangement between the company and its creditors or any class of those creditors." The intention of the programme is to allow for "simpler, faster, and lower-cost proceedings to assist micro and small companies in need of winding up or restructuring" (Ministry of Law, 2023[32]). The simplified programme consists of a Simplified Debt Restructuring Programme (restructuring of debts and possible rehabilitation for viable businesses) and a Simplified Winding Up Programme (where non-viable businesses are wound up in an orderly manner).

Some countries have additional provisions in their insolvency frameworks. For example, in Bangladesh, where there is default by a bond issuer and subject to a declaration of bankruptcy by the appropriate court, the court will appoint a liquidator who will liquidate the assets and pay out the obligations as per the seniority of the bondholder along with other claimholders. This court-settled liquidation process may take several years or even decades to finally be executed completely (Government of Bangladesh, 1994[33]; 1997[34]).

In 15 jurisdictions there is a system to record and/or identify bondholders (China, Hong Kong (China), India, Indonesia, Japan, Lao PDR, Malaysia, Mongolia, Pakistan, Philippines, Singapore, Sri Lanka, Chinese Taipei, Thailand and Viet Nam) (Figure 5.4, Panel B). One of the key challenges in a restructuring or insolvency procedures relating to a corporate bond is the identification of bondholders. To name a few systems, the one in Hong Kong (China) records and identifies bondholders for the bonds lodged with the Central Monetary Markets Unit (CMU) operated by the Hong Kong Monetary Authority (HKMA). This is run by the Central Moneymarkets Unit, which is owned and operated by the Hong Kong Monetary Authority. This is the clearing and settlement system in Hong Kong for debt securities denominated in Hong Kong dollars and other major currencies (HKMA, 2023[35]). In Thailand, there is a similar registration system, which was introduced by the Bank of Thailand in 2021. This requires investors to be registered before investing in Thai bonds. The aim of the system is for the Bank of Thailand to have "comprehensive, correct, and readily available data with regards to investment in Thai bond market to ensure proper market surveillance and timely policy implementation" (Bank of Thailand, 2023[36]).

5.2.3. Role of covenants in corporate bond contracts

Covenants in bond contracts are the main corporate governance tool of bondholders. Certain provisions in corporate bonds and other debt contracts may significantly limit the discretion of management and shareholders, such as covenants that restrict dividend payouts, require creditors' approval for the divestment of major assets, or penalise debtors if financial leverage exceeds a predetermined threshold. Moreover, under financial stress but before bankruptcy, companies may choose to negotiate a waiver of compliance with a covenant, when existing creditors may require changes in the business. As a consequence, the timely disclosure of material information on debt contracts, including the impact of material risks related to a covenant breach and the likelihood of their occurrence, in accordance with applicable standards, is necessary for investors to understand a company's business risks." The revised G20/OECD Principles of Corporate Governance provide in Principle VI specific guidance for listed issuers with respect to disclosure, transparency and debt contracts, including the risk of non-compliance with covenants (OECD, 2023[17]).

Notably, **all jurisdictions require material information disclosure on covenants**. Additionally, Figure 5.5 provides information on the most commonly included covenants in corporate bond contracts during the last five years. Across the 19 jurisdictions the most common covenants over the past five years were considered to be "leverage restrictions", "secured debt restrictions" and "subordinated debt restrictions". The least common were "dividend payment restrictions", "cross-default provisions" and "sale and lease-back restrictions". This contrasts the findings from some other jurisdictions such as the United States where the three covenant types that were used in approximately 90% of investment and non-investment grade bond contracts in 2020 were cross-default provisions, merger restrictions and asset sale restrictions (de Oliveira, Magnusson and Mulazimoglu, 2022[8]). The results also highlight differences across jurisdictions in the use of covenants. For example, "asset sale restrictions" and "investment policy restrictions" were considered to be common in seven jurisdictions and not common in six jurisdictions.

Figure 5.5. Use of selected covenants in corporate bond contracts during the last 5 years

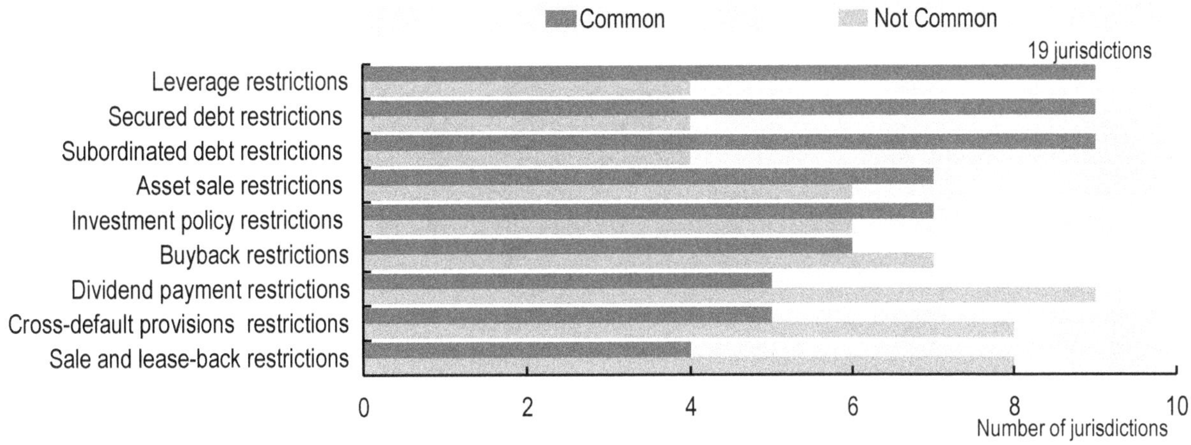

Source: OECD Survey on Access to Corporate Bond Markets for Growth Companies in Asia, see Annex B for details.

5.2.4. Changes in bondholder rights

The OECD Survey also assessed the perspective of regulators on whether there had been an increase or decrease in bondholder rights in their jurisdiction over the previous five years. While most jurisdictions did not have data-based metrics to respond to this question **11 jurisdictions considered that there had not been a change in bondholder rights over the past five years** (Figure 5.6, Panel A). **In 7 jurisdictions, the perception was that there had been an increase in bondholder rights**, while no jurisdiction perceived a decrease in bondholder rights over this period.

Figure 5.6. Bondholder rights

Source: OECD Survey on Access to Corporate Bond Markets for Growth Companies in Asia, see Annex B for details.

An example of a jurisdiction taking steps to improve bondholder rights is India. In India, SEBI has taken various steps to develop the corporate bond market as well as to protect the interest of investors. For instance, the declaration of information about why the audit is conducted and who is doing the audit is required to improve the information available to and the decision making of bondholders. There are now requirements for an e-voting facility for bondholders who have a digital account to hold and trade financial securities (known as a "demat account"), so that they can vote from anywhere. The Securities and Exchange Board of India has mandated disclosures pertaining to analyst meetings, investor meetings and conference calls so that information asymmetries and information sharing with only a few investors can be eliminated (SEBI, 2020[37]; 2015[38]). There are also now provisions pertaining to the appointment of a nominee director to protect the interests of bondholders (SEBI, 2023[39]).

Another example of a measure to improve bondholder rights is in Bangladesh, where the Securities and Exchange Commission is developing a bond management platform to supervise and ensure the matters related to coupon payment, default mechanism, due diligence of bondholder rights in case of distress or default by the borrower. Mongolia also made changes in 2021 and 2022, so that a debt instrument must have a collateral, a trustee or guarantee, or the bond issuer must be credit-rated by a locally or internationally recognised agency in order to secure the payment obligations of both the privately and publicly offered debt instruments and to protect bondholder rights (Mongolian Financial Regulatory Commission, 2021[40]; 2022[41]).

Relatedly, the Securities and Exchange Commission of Thailand sent a circular letter relating to the expectation of bondholder representative (trustee) duties which solidified the rights of bondholder. In addition, there were a series of changes in 2019 that strengthened bondholder rights, relating to: issuer's duties (e.g. financial statement must be sent to the bondholder representative (trustee) and they must be informed of an event of default without delay); restrictions in covenants (e.g. on leverage and dividends payable); additional events added to default terms (e.g. where debtors are unable to comply with financial covenants and stopping operations which might have significant impact); and the implementation of additional measures after a bond default (such as auto-acceleration in the case of insolvency/rehabilitation).

5.2.5. Role of industry associations

Industry-led bodies or associations can play a valuable role in promoting the development of markets, lifting the standards of the industry, improving the products offered to investors, and creating a corporate bond market landscape that supports bondholder rights. **In 11 jurisdictions there is an industry-led body or industry association that is active in relation to the corporate bond market** (China, India, Japan, Korea, Malaysia, Mongolia, Philippines, Singapore, Chinese Taipei, Thailand and Viet Nam) (Figure 5.6, Panel B). The role of these associations varies across jurisdictions. Seven jurisdictions (China, Japan, Korea, Mongolia, Chinese Taipei, Thailand and Viet Nam) reported that the body has a self-regulatory role, seven jurisdictions (China, Japan, Korea, Malaysia, Philippines, Chinese Taipei and Thailand) reported that the body has a role in promoting and developing the debt securities market, and one jurisdiction (Philippines) reported that there is a regional body or association with a role in promoting and developing the debt securities market in the region.

One example is the Thai Bond Association, whose "main purposes are to be a self-regulatory organisation for a fair and efficient operation of the bond market and to be an information centre for the Thai bond market. It also plays functional roles in market development, market convention and standards and being [a] Bond Pricing agency for the industry" (ThaiBMA, 2023[42]). The Thai Bond Association has also published a template for corporate bond contracts to assist the industry with standardising terms and conditions (ThaiBMA, 2023[43]).

While Thailand has a body focusing on the bond market, in other jurisdictions this is covered by associations with a broader remit. For example, in India, there are bodies like the Federation of Indian Chambers of Commerce & Industry, Confederation of Indian industries, Associated Chambers of Commerce and Industry who are involved in various corporate matters, including the bond market.

In addition to the role played by jurisdiction-specific associations relevant work is also conducted via regional and global trade associations and other organisations, for example, the Asia Securities Industry and Financial Markets Association (ASIFMA), the International Capital Market Association (ICMA), and the Asian Development Bank (ADB), among others. They play an important role in promoting the development of bond markets in the region and internationally, sharing best practices and leveraging international experiences. For example, ASIFMA has launched initiatives on critical parts of the market such as bond issuance, credit ratings, transparency and electronification, tax and compliance. Another example in the region is the AsianBondsOnline web portal, that is an ASEAN+3 Initiative supported by the Asian Development Bank, which is a source of information on bond markets in emerging East Asia (ADB, 2023[44]).

In contrast, Singapore reported that the industry-led body active in relation to the corporate bond market does not have a self-regulatory role, and eight jurisdictions (Australia, Bangladesh, Cambodia, Hong Kong (China), Indonesia, Lao PDR, Pakistan and Sri Lanka) reported that there is not an industry-led body or industry association that is active in relation to the corporate bond market in their jurisdiction.

References

ADB (2023), *AsianBondsOnline*, https://asianbondsonline.adb.org/. [44]

ADB (2018), *ASEAN+3 Bond Market Guide 2018: Republic of Korea*, https://doi.org/10.22617/TCS189302-2. [7]

Bank of Thailand (2023), *Bond Investor Registration*, https://www.bot.or.th/en/our-roles/financial-markets/Financial-Market-Development-and-Standards/Elevating-Financial-Market-Standards/BIR.html. [36]

Bergthaler, W. et al. (2015), *Tackling Small and Medium Enterprise Problem Loans in Europe*, https://www.imf.org/en/Publications/Staff-Discussion-Notes/Issues/2016/12/31/Tackling-Small-and-Medium-Enterprise-Problem-Loans-in-Europe-42614. [27]

Brodie, S. (2017), "Bonds and restructurings: corporate bond considerations in the design of debt restructuring frameworks in emerging market economies", *Law and Financial Markets Review*, Vol. 11/2-3, pp. 2-117-125, https://doi.org/10.1080/17521440.2017.137913. [9]

Çelik, S., G. Demirtaş and M. Isaksson (2020), *Corporate Bond Market Trends, Emerging Risks and Monetary Policy*, OECD, Paris, https://www.oecd.org/corporate/Corporate-Bond-Market-Trends-Emerging-Risks-and-Monetary-Policy.htm. [1]

Clifford Chance (2018), *A guide to Asia Pacific restructuring and insolvancy procedures*, https://www.cliffordchance.com/content/dam/cliffordchance/briefings/2013/08/a-guide-to-asia-pacific-restructuring-and-insolvency-procedures.pdf. [21]

de Oliveira, C., C. Magnusson and T. Mulazimoglu (2022), "The role and rights of debtholders in corporate governance", *OECD Corporate Governance Working Papers*, No. 23, OECD Publishing, Paris, https://doi.org/10.1787/d6b7cca5-en. [8]

Dutra Araujo, J. et al. (2022), *Departmental Paper: Policy Options for Supporting and Restructuring Firms Hit by the COVID-19 Crisis*, IMF, https://doi.org/10.5089/9781513593463.087. [28]

ESCAP (2017), *Korean Experience in Credit Guarantee Scheme to Enhance Financial Accessibility of MSMEs*, United Nations, https://www.unescap.org/sites/default/files/Panel%202-2.%20KODIT_Mr.%20Jong-goo%20Lee.pdf. [45]

ESMA (2024), *CRA Authorisation*, https://www.esma.europa.eu/credit-rating-agencies/cra-authorisation (accessed on November 2023). [6]

Fitch Ratings (2020), *Unsuccessful Distressed Debt Exchanges May Lead to Bankruptcy*, https://www.fitchratings.com/research/corporate-finance/unsuccessful-distressed-debt-exchanges-may-lead-to-bankruptcy-28-09-2020. [25]

FSB (2022), *Thematic Review on Out-of-Court Corporate Debt Workouts: Peer Review Report*, https://www.fsb.org/wp-content/uploads/P090522.pdf. [26]

Fund, K. (ed.) (2019), *2019 Annual Report*, http://www.shinbo.co.kr/annualMgt/annual_20200706182206.pdf. [2]

Gorvernment of Chinese Taipei (2021), *Company Act*, https://law.moj.gov.tw/ENG/LawClass/LawAll.aspx?pcode=J0080001. [15]

Government of Australia (2020), *Corporations Amendment (Corporate Insolvency Reforms) Act 2020 (No. 130)*, https://www.legislation.gov.au/Details/C2020A00130. [30]

Government of Australia (2001), *Corporations Act 2001 (No. 50)*, https://www.legislation.gov.au/Details/C2023C00194. [22]

Government of Bangladesh (1997), *Bankruptcy Act, 1997 (No. 10)*, http://bdlaws.minlaw.gov.bd/act-812.html?lang=en. [34]

Government of Bangladesh (1994), *Companies Act, 1994 (No. 18)*, http://bdlaws.minlaw.gov.bd/act-788.html. [33]

Government of Indonesia (2023), *Financial Sector Development and Strengthening Law 2023 (No. 4, P2SK Law)*, https://jdih.kemenkeu.go.id/download/58fac07c-7165-4c55-882d-965687f8090b/UU4TAHUN2023.pdf. [12]

Government of Japan (1999), *Civil Rehabilitation Act (No. 225)*, https://www.japaneselawtranslation.go.jp/en/laws/view/125/en. [23]

Government of Malaysia (2007), *Capital Markets and Services Act 2007 (Act 671)*, https://www.sc.com.my/regulation/acts/capital-markets-and-services-act-2007. [13]

Government of Singapore (2018), *Insolvency, Restructuring and Dissolution Act 1998*, https://sso.agc.gov.sg/Act/IRDA2018/Uncommenced/20231028?DocDate=20221028&ValidDt=20231101. [31]

Government of the Philippines (2010), *Financial Rehabilitation and Insolvency Act of 2010 (Act No. 10142)*, https://lawphil.net/statutes/repacts/ra2010/ra_10142_2010.html. [20]

HKMA (2023), *Principles for Financial Market Infrastructures Disclosure for Central Moneymarkets Unit*, Hong Kong Monetary Authority, https://www.hkma.gov.hk/media/eng/doc/key-functions/financial-infrastructure/infrastructure/cmu_disclosure_framework.pdf. [35]

Hong Kong Monetary Authority (2020), *Alternative credit scoring of micro-, small and medium sized enterprises*, https://www.hkma.gov.hk/media/eng/doc/key-functions/financial-infrastructure/alternative_credit_scoring.pdf. [3]

IOSCO (2015), “IOSCO Code of Conduct Fundamentals for Credit Rating Agencies”, https://www.iosco.org/library/pubdocs/pdf/IOSCOPD482.pdf. [4]

Japan Credit Rating Agency, Ltd (2023), *Association of Credit Rating Agencies in Asia (ACRAA)*, https://www.jcr.co.jp/en/service/international/acraa/. [5]

Ministry of Law (2023), *SIP FAQ*, https://io.mlaw.gov.sg/corporate-insolvency/sip-faq/#:~:text=The%20SIP%20seeks%20to%20provide,start%20on%2029%20Jan%202021. [32]

Mongolian Financial Regulatory Commission (2022), *Regulation on the Registration of Securities in OTC Market (No. 360)*, https://legalinfo.mn/mn/detail?lawId=16530694451051. [41]

Mongolian Financial Regulatory Commission (2021), *Regulation on Securities Registration*, http://www.frc.mn/resource/frc/Document/2022/12/26/zkow2aacboltj2zc/Regulation%20on%20Securities%20Registration.pdf. [40]

Nishimura & Asahi (2011), *An introduction to court procedures for insolvency in Japan*, https://www.nishimura.com/en/knowledge/publications/20110408-39201#:~:text=The%20purpose%20of%20the%20civil,to%20both%20individuals%20and%20corporations. [24]

OECD (2023), *G20/OECD Principles of Corporate Governance 2023*, OECD Publishing, Paris, https://doi.org/10.1787/ed750b30-en. [17]

OECD (2021), *The Future of Corporate Governance in Capital Markets Following the COVID-19 Crisis*, Corporate Governance, OECD Publishing, Paris, https://doi.org/10.1787/efb2013c-en. [19]

OJK (2020), *Regulation No. 20/POJK.04/2020 Concerning Trustee Contracts for Debt Securities and/or Sukuk*, https://ojk.go.id/id/regulasi/Documents/Pages/Kontrak-Perwaliamanatan-Efek-Bersifat-Utang-dan-atau-Sukuk--/POJK%2020-2020.pdf#search=20%2FPOJK%2E04%2F2020. [10]

OJK (2020), *Regulation No. 57 /POJK.04/2020 Offering securities through technology-based crowdfunding services*, https://ojk.go.id/id/regulasi/Documents/Pages/Penawaran-Efek-Melalui-Layanan-Urun-Dana-Berbasis-Teknologi-Informasi/pojk%2057%20-%2004%20-%202020.pdf#search=No%2E%2020%2FPOJK%2E04%2F2020. [11]

SC Malaysia (2020), *Guidelines on Trust Deeds*, https://www.sc.com.my/regulation/guidelines/bonds-and-sukuk. [14]

SEBI (2023), *SEBI Circular SEBI/HO/DDHS/POD1/P/CIR/2023/112: Appointment of Director nominated by the Debenture Trustee on boards of issuers*, https://www.sebi.gov.in/legal/circulars/jul-2023/appointment-of-director-nominated-by-the-debenture-trustee-on-boards-of-issuers_73439.html. [39]

SEBI (2020), *Report on disclosures pertaining to analyst meets, investor meets and conference calls*, https://www.sebi.gov.in/reports-and-statistics/reports/nov-2020/report-on-disclosures-pertaining-to-analyst-meets-investor-meets-and-conference-calls_48208.html. [37]

SEBI (2015), *Listing Obligations and Disclosure Requirements) Regulations*, https://www.sebi.gov.in/legal/regulations/jul-2022/securities-and-exchange-board-of-india-listing-obligations-and-disclosure-requirements-regulations-2015-last-amended-on-july-25-2022-_61405.html. [38]

ThaiBMA (2023), *About the Thai Bond Market Association (ThaiBMA)*, https://www.thaibma.or.th/EN/About/Background.aspx#:~:text=Its%20main%20purposes%20are%20to,Pricing%20agency%20for%20the%20industry. (accessed on 2023). [42]

ThaiBMA (2023), *Regulatory Framework: The issuance and offering of debt securities*, http://www.thaibma.or.th/EN/Rule/RegulatoryEN.aspx (accessed on 19 September 2023). [43]

World Bank (2016), *Principles for Effective Insolvency and Creditor/Debtor Regimes*, https://documents1.worldbank.org/curated/en/518861467086038847/pdf/106399-WP-REVISED-PUBLIC-ICR-Principle-Final-Hyperlinks-revised-Latest.pdf. [16]

World Bank (2014), *Debt Resolution and Business Exit: Insolvency Reform for Credit, Entrepreneurship, and Growth*, https://documents.worldbank.org/en/publication/documents-reports/documentdetail/912041468178733220/debt-resolution-and-business-exit-insolvency-reform-for-credit-entrepreneurship-and-growth. [18]

World Bank Group (2021), *Overview of Insolvency and Debt Restructuring Reforms in Response to the COVID-19 Pandemic and Past Financial Crises: Lessons for Emerging Markets*, https://documents1.worldbank.org/curated/en/182341615352260595/pdf/Overview-of-Insolvency-and-Debt-Restructuring-Reforms-in-Response-to-the-COVID-19-Pandemic-and-Past-Financial-Crises-Lessons-for-Emerging-Markets.pdf. [29]

Notes

[1] Bangladesh, Cambodia, Indonesia, Japan, Korea, Malaysia, Mongolia, Pakistan and Philippines.

[2] While international CRAs could provide services to markets in almost all jurisdictions, here refers in the cases where there is a branch of an international CRA or domestic CRAs are affiliated with international CRAs through their stakes in domestic CRAs.

[3] Australia, China, Hong Kong (China), India, Korea, Singapore, Sri Lanka, Chinese Taipei, Thailand and Viet Nam

[4] The FIBEN system collects and integrates all available financial information about individual firms and provides credit scores to investors or lenders for a certain fee. The system is accessible for credit institutions, insurance companies and asset management companies, among others. The central bank also performs an independent risk analysis of French enterprises that allows lenders to assess credit risks of potential clients at a low cost, which facilitates access to finance, in particular for SMEs.

[5] The KODIT is the one of the largest single entity credit guarantee institutions in the world (ESCAP, 2017[45]). It introduced the primary collateralized bond obligations guarantee in July 2000 to support Korean bond market conditions that were undermined by the currency crisis that started in the late 1990s. The main goal was to help restore the confidence of the market participants and to stabilise the disrupted Korean corporate bonds market.

[6] SME Corporation Malaysia operates under the Ministry of Entrepreneur & Cooperatives Development (MECD). Further information is available on the website of SME Corp. Malaysia.

[7] Alternatively, there are three CRAs that are specialised in providing credit ratings for SMEs and mid-tier companies. Notably, Credit Bureau Malaysia (CBM) is the country's main credit bureau that provides credit reporting and credit scoring services for both individuals and businesses. Their services include credit reports, credit scores, and credit monitoring. Also, CTOS Data Systems Sdn Bhd (CTOS) provides credit reports and credit scores for businesses of all sizes. They also offer other services such as business background checks, fraud prevention and risk management. Credit Scan Malaysia (Dun & Bradstreet) is a global provider of business information and credit ratings. Dun & Bradstreet offer a range of credit reporting and risk management services for SMEs and mid-tier companies, including credit reports, credit scores, and credit monitoring.

[8] For detail see Regulation (CE) N°. 1060/2009 of the European Parliament and of the Council on the credit rating agencies adopted in 2009, article 23, section I.

[9] For details see Credit Rating Agency Reform Act, article 15E, sub paragraph c), section (2).

[10] While out-of-court workouts or restructurings can occur in any jurisdiction, the nine jurisdictions mentioned here have incorporated provisions related to these systems into their legal or regulatory frameworks.

Annex A. Definition of growth companies in selected regions and jurisdictions

Jurisdiction	Growth company / SME definition
Australia	Definition by the Australian Bureau of Statistics: • Small business: fewer than 20 employees and turnover less than AUD 2 million (c. USD 1.3 million) • Medium business: 20-199 employees Definition by the Corporations Act: • Small company: no more than 50 employees, annual turnover less than AUD 25 million (c. USD 16.0 million), and assets under AUD 12.5 million (c. USD 8.0 million) Definition by the taxation laws: • Small business: turnover less than AUD 10 million (c. USD 6.4 million) • Medium business: turnover between AUD 10 million (c. USD 6.4 million) – AUD 250 million (c. USD 159.8 million).
Bangladesh	• A paid-up capital between BDT 500 billion (c. USD 5 million) – BDT 5 billion (c. USD 50 million)
China	• For agriculture industry: turnover of less than RMB 20 million (c. USD 2.7 million) • For information technology industry: turnover of less than RMB 1 billion (c. USD 137 million) • For leasing business industry: less than 300 employees
Hong Kong (China)	• Manufacturing establishments: employees fewer than 100 • Non-manufacturing establishments: employees fewer than 50
India	• Small company: Investment in plant and machinery or equipment less than INR 100 million (c. USD 1.2 million) and turnover less than INR 500 million (c. USD 6.0 million) • Medium company: Investment in plant and machinery or equipment less than INR 500 million (c. USD 6.0 million) and turnover less than INR 2.5 billion (c. USD 30 million)
Indonesia	• Small company: Total assets no more than IDR 50 billion (c. USD 3.2 million). Not controlled by middle/large scale companies or companies with assets more than IDR 250 billion (c. USD 16.2 million) • Medium company: Total assets no more than IDR 250 billion (c. USD 16.2 million). Not controlled by large scale companies or companies with assets more than IDR 250 billion (c. USD 16.2 million)
Japan	• Manufacturing: less than 300 employees or capital less than JPY 300 million (c. USD 2.0 million) • Wholesale: less than 100 employees or capital less than JPY 100 million (c. USD 0.6 million) • Service: less than 100 employees or capital less than JPY 50 million (c. USD 0.3 million) • Retail: less than 50 employees or capital less than JPY 50 million (c. USD 0.3 million)
Korea	• Total asset less than KRW 500 billion (c. USD 377 million) • Actual separation of management and ownership, a company does not fall into the following categories: o A company belongs to a conglomerate o A company with total assets at least KRW 500 billion (c. USD 377 million) and the largest shareholder owing 30% or more of the total outstanding shares.
Lao PDR	Meeting at least one of the following three criteria: • Small company: Less than 19 employees or total assets less than LAK 250 million (c. USD 12.5 thousand) or turnover less than LAK 400 million (c. USD 22.5 thousand) • Medium company: Less than 99 employees or total assets less than LAK 1 billion (c. USD 50 thousand) or turnover LAK 1 billion (c. USD 50 thousand)
Malaysia	• Manufacturing: less than 200 employees or turnover less than RM 50 million (c. USD 10.6 million) • Service and other sectors: less than 75 employees or turnover less than RM 20 million (c. USD 4.2 million)
Mongolia	• Micro company: less than 10 employees and annual sales less than MNT 300 million (c. USD 86.9 thousand) • Small company: between 10-50 employees and annual sales between MNT 300 million (c. USD 86.9 thousand) -1 billion (c. USD 0.3 million) • Medium company: between 50-5200 employees and annual sales between MNT 1 billion (c. USD 0.3 million) -25 billion (c. USD 7.2 million)

Jurisdiction	Growth company / SME definition
Pakistan	SME definition: Meeting at least one of the following three criteria: • Small company: (1) Paid-up capital less than PKR 10 million (c. USD 33.8 thousand), (2) turnover less than PKR 100 million (c. USD 0.3 million), or (3) less than 250 employees • Medium company: (1) Paid-up capital less than PKR 200 million (c. USD 0.7 million), (2) turnover less than PKR 1 billion (c. USD 3.3 million), or (3) employees between 250-750 Growth company definition: • A company meeting the eligibility criteria for listing at the Growth Enterprise Market. The listing criteria include: (1) post issue paid up capital of at least PKR 25 million (c. USD 86.4 thousand), (2) the issue size shall not be less than 5 million shares and PKR 50 million (c. USD 0.2 million)
Philippines	• Micro company: Employees between 1-9 and total assets less than PHP 3 million (c. USD 52.9 thousand) • Small company: Employees between 10-99 and total assets between PHP 3 million (c. USD 52.9 thousand) - PHP 15 million (c. USD 0.3 million) • Medium company: Employees between 100-199 and total assets PHP 15 million (c. USD 0.3 million) - PHP 100 million (c. USD 1.8 million)
Singapore	• Less than 200 employees and turnover less than SGD 100 million (c. USD 73.3 million)
Chinese Taipei	• Less than 200 employees and paid-in capital less than TWD100 million (c. USD 3.1 million)
Thailand	Small company: • Manufacturing: Less than 50 employees and turnover less than THB 100 million (c. USD 2.8 million) • Wholesale, retail, and service: Less than 30 employees and turnover less than THB 50 million (c. USD 1.4 million) Medium company: • Manufacturing: Less than 200 employees and turnover less than THB 500 million (c. USD 13.9 million) • Wholesale, retail, and service: Less than 100 employees and turnover less than THB 300 million (c. USD 8.3 million)
Viet Nam	Micro company: • Agriculture, forestry, and fishing: Less than 10 employees and, total revenue less than VND 3 billion (c. USD 0.1 million) or total capital less than VND 3 billion (c. USD 0.1 million) • Trade and services: Less than 10 employees and, total revenue less than VND 10 billion (c. USD 0.4 million) or total capital less than VND 3 billion (c. USD 0.1 million) Small company: • Agriculture, forestry, and fishing: Employees between 11-100 and, total revenue less than VND 50 billion (c. USD 2.0 million) or total capital less than VND 20 billion (c. USD 0.8 million) • Trade and services: Employees between 11-50 and, total revenue less than VND 100 billion (c. USD 4.1 million) or total capital less than VND 50 billion (c. USD 2.0 million) Medium company: • Agriculture, forestry, and fishing: Employees between 101-200 and total revenue less than VND 300 billion (c. USD 12.3 million) or total capital less than VND 100 billion (c. USD 4.1 million) • Trade and services: Employees between 51-100 and, total revenue less than VND 300 billion (c. USD 12.3 million) or total capital less than VND 100 billion (c. USD 4.1 million)
EU	• Micro company: Employees less than 10, and turnover less than EUR 2 million (c. USD 2.2 million) or balance sheet total less than EUR 2 million (c. USD 2.2 million) • Small company: Employees between 10-49, and turnover less than EUR 10 million (c. USD 11 million) or balance sheet total less than EUR 10 million (c. USD 11 million) • Medium company: Employees between 50-249, and turnover less than EUR 50 million (c. USD 54.9 million) or balance sheet total less than EUR 43 million (c. USD 47.2 million)
OECD	• Micro company: Employees less than 10 • Small company: Employees between 10-49 • Medium company: Employees between 50-249

Note: Cambodia and Sri Lanka do not have a definition for growth companies or SMEs. Local currencies are converted to USD using the exchange rate from Bloomberg and/or central banks on September 20, 2023.
Source: Australian Bureau of Statistics, Australian Taxation Office, Lao National Chamber of Commerce and Industry, SME Corporation Malaysia, Pakistan Stock Exchange, Philippine Statistics Authority, The Supreme People's Court of the Socialist Republic of Viet Nam, European Commission, OECD statistics and OECD Survey on Access to Corporate Bond Markets for Growth Companies in Asia.

Annex B. Methodology for data collection and classification

A. OECD Survey on Access to Corporate Bond Markets for Growth Companies in Asia

The OECD conducted an extensive survey, the "*OECD Survey on Access to Corporate Bond Markets for Growth Companies in Asia*" (OECD Survey) that was answered by 19 jurisdictions namely: Australia, Bangladesh, Cambodia, Hong Kong (China), India, Indonesia, Japan, Korea, Lao PDR, Malaysia, Mongolia, Pakistan, China, Philippines, Singapore, Sri Lanka, Chinese Taipei, Thailand and Viet Nam. The survey was conducted in the first half of 2023.

Among many other things, the OECD Survey explored the practices in these jurisdictions relating to the corporate bond issuance procedure, measures to support access to corporate bond markets for companies, tax treatment of corporate bonds, marketplaces for listing and trading corporate bonds, credit rating requirements, bondholder rights and barriers to the development of corporate bond markets.

B. Corporate bond data

Data presented on corporate bonds are based on OECD calculations using data obtained from LSEG that provides international deal-level data on new publicly and privately issued corporate bonds that are underwritten by an investment bank. The database provides a detailed set of information for each corporate bond issue, including the identity, nationality and sector of the issuer; the type, interest rate structure, maturity date and rating category of the bond; and the amount of and use of proceeds obtained from the issue.

Convertible bonds, deals that were registered but not consummated, preferred shares, sukuk bonds, bonds with an original maturity less than or equal to 1 year or an issue size less than USD 1 million are excluded from the dataset. The industry classification is carried out based on LSEG Business and Industry Classifications. The country breakdown is carried out based on the issuer's country of domicile. Yearly issuance amounts initially collected in USD were adjusted by 2022 US Consumer Price Index (CPI). Information provided is adjusted by CPI and presented in 2022 USD.

Given that a significant portion of bonds are issued on foreign markets, it is not possible to assign such issues to a single market. For this reason, the country breakdown is carried out based on the jurisdiction of domicile of the issuer.

The OECD definition of a "growth company" is a small and medium-sized enterprise (SME) with the potential to rapidly expand, create jobs, increase productivity, push the frontiers of innovation and challenge the status quo with new products and business models. In this report, corporate bonds issued by growth companies refers to issuances of less than USD 50 million.

Australia participated in the survey without being an Asian jurisdiction. Data referring to Asia as a region, for simplicity, includes Australia, and the following 18 Asian jurisdictions: Bangladesh, Cambodia, China, Hong Kong (China), India, Indonesia, Japan, Korea, Lao PDR, Malaysia, Mongolia, Pakistan, Philippines, Singapore, Sri Lanka, Chinese Taipei, Thailand and Viet Nam.

Rating data

LSEG provides rating information from the three leading rating agencies: S&P, Fitch and Moody's. For each bond that has rating information in the dataset, a value of 1 is assigned to the lowest credit quality rating (C) and 21 is assigned to the highest credit quality rating (AAA for S&P and Fitch and Aaa for Moody's). There are eleven non-investment grade categories: five from C (C to CCC+); and six from B (B- to BB+). There are ten investment grade categories: three from B (BBB- to BBB+); and seven from A (A- to AAA).

If ratings from multiple rating agencies are available for a given issue, their average is used. Some issues in the dataset, on the other hand, do not have rating information available. For such issues, the average rating of all bonds issued by the same issuer in the same year (t) is assigned. If the issuer has no rated bonds in year t, year t-1 and year t-2 are also considered, respectively. This procedure increases the number of rated bonds in the dataset and hence improves the representativeness of rating-based analyses. When differentiating between investment and non-investment grade bonds, the final rating is rounded to the closest integer and issues with a rounded rating less than or equal to 11 are classified as non-investment grade.

Early redemption data

When calculating the outstanding amount of corporate bonds in a given year, issues that are no longer outstanding due to being redeemed earlier than their maturity are deducted. The early redemption data and cover bonds that have been redeemed early due to being repaid via final default distribution, called, liquidated, put or repurchased are obtained from LSEG. The early redemption data is merged with the primary corporate bond market data via international securities identification numbers (i.e. ISINs).

C. Market capitalisation and number of listed companies' data

The main source of market capitalisation information provided in Chapter 2 is LSEG. Data is collected at the end of 2022 in current USD, thus no currency nor inflation adjustments are needed. The dataset includes the 38 998 non-financial listed companies. With the aim of including only listed companies on the main stock exchanges, the following securities are excluded:

- non-primary listings
- companies listed on multilateral trading facilities
- companies listed on OTC markets
- companies listed on alternative markets primarily targeting SMEs.

www.ingramcontent.com/pod-product-compliance
Lightning Source LLC
Chambersburg PA
CBHW061224240926
51846CB00006B/1342
* 9 7 8 9 2 6 4 5 3 4 4 1 4 *